To Sheila Melvin

from

John Stuttard

T
NEV
RC

THE NEW SILK ROAD

Secrets of
Business Success
in China Today

JOHN B. STUTTARD

Foreword by
JAMES J. SCHIRO

John Wiley & Sons, Inc.
New York • Chichester • Weinheim • Brisbane • Singapore • Toronto

ISBN 0-471-37722-8

Printed in the United States of America.
10 9 8 7 6 5 4 3 2 1

*To my wife, Lesley, for her love, support,
and patience during our five years in China*

Acknowledgments

During my five years in the People's Republic of China, I received invaluable advice and support from my colleagues at Pricewaterhouse Coopers. I wish to thank four in particular: Roderick Chalmers and Marina Wong in Hong Kong, Gordon Barrass in London, and Ruby Chin in Shanghai. I also wish to thank Kent Watson, my successor as chairman of PricewaterhouseCoopers China, for his wise counsel and friendship since the announcement of the merger of Coopers & Lybrand and Price Waterhouse. I was delighted to come in touch, through our merger, with a new group of partners who know China well.

The views expressed in this book by my clients and colleagues represent, to my mind, the best available sources of advice on how to succeed in business in China. I am grateful to the 11 chairmen I interviewed for the time they set aside for our discussions. I am also grateful to my assistants in Beijing and London, respectively Cathy Jiang and Liz Mills, who transcribed tapes of interviews; and to David Lascelles, formerly a senior journalist with *Financial Times;* and to my wife, Lesley, for reading and commenting on early drafts.

The following of my fellow partners read the chapter "Reflections" and provided helpful comments: Paul Batchelor, Johnny Chen, Paul Gillis, Joe Ragg, and Kent Watson. Particular thanks go to Professor Ken DeWoskin, a Sinologist at the University of Michigan at Ann Arbor and a partner in PricewaterhouseCoopers China, for his comprehensive input based on a lifetime's study and experience of China. I would also like to thank Bill Dauphinais and

Roger Lipsey of PricewaterhouseCoopers New York, who gave the text a final review and arranged its publication.

Finally, I wish to express my appreciation to Jim Schiro, chief executive of PricewaterhouseCoopers International, for giving me the inspiration to undertake this book and for writing the Foreword.

Contents

Foreword

The origin of this book was a conversation in Beijing, little more than a year ago. I knew that John Stuttard, the senior Pricewater-houseCoopers partner in China, had something more than thorough experience of the Chinese business environment. He could shape complex facts into a clear and insightful whole, and nothing was lost in the transition from the spoken to the written word. I encouraged him to write a book about the ground rules and fine points of doing business in China today. I was sure that our clients and many readers worldwide would value such a book.

Naturally, I didn't believe that a book could "tell all"—experience is the teacher, nowhere more so than in China. But if anyone could help foreign companies already in China or considering China—if anyone could wisely prepare foreign executives for China—it was John. We talked through the challenges. This book is the result.

To assemble the many-sided view that he felt was necessary, John adopted the strategy of interviewing outstanding foreign business leaders active in many different industries in China. Blending his own thought and experience with those of his interviewees, he has crafted a book that should be read by everyone who is seriously interested in business in China. You will find here the voices and insights of people who are responsible for great assets and even greater corporate aspirations in China, people who know their way. They understand the unique texture of Chinese civilization, history, government, and business culture. They have patiently built relationships and businesses—and successes.

PricewaterhouseCoopers is working today with many companies already in China, or approaching China, to meet their diverse needs and provide solutions at every stage of negotiation and business development. For our clients present and future, and for Chinese nationals active in business and at the interface between business and government, we are committed to providing authentic thought leadership—by which we mean information and ideas, insights and counsel that help good, things to happen. This new book represents, in the full sense of the word, thought leadership from PricewaterhouseCoopers. It is the very best introduction I have encountered to doing business in today's China. We are proud to be associated with it, and grateful to John Stuttard and to the group of senior business leaders who share their experience and insights in these pages.

James J. Schiro

Introduction

Noel Coward wrote *Private Lives* in Shanghai in 1929, while staying at the newly completed Cathay Hotel on the Bund. The ocean-going liners and yachts gliding up the Huang Pu River gave him a backdrop for the play's romantic comedy. At that time, Shanghai was Asia's greatest commercial, industrial, and financial center. It was to remain so until the Japanese occupation, from 1937, ended an era of extraordinary adventure and financial success. Then, after the Revolution in 1949, Shanghai seemed to lie dormant, only to rise again in recent years like a phoenix to China's awakening dragon.

I first visited the People's Republic of China (PRC) in January 1981. While working in Hong Kong, I had signed up for a week-long package tour with the China International Travel Service—the only way, at that time, to visit the country. China had just begun to welcome tourists after a 30-year hiatus during which the PRC was effectively closed to the outside world. My memories are of men and women dressed in dark green or navy blue Mao suits, dimly lit streets, basic hotels, an absence of cars and taxis, but forests of bicycles—and people who were friendly, albeit inquisitive and wary of the "big noses," a term sometimes used by Chinese to describe foreigners.

Thirteen years later, in January 1994, I participated in a seminar organized by British Invisibles, a group that promotes financial and professional services for the City of London and The London Stock Exchange. We visited Beijing and Shanghai. The country had been transformed. New buildings had sprung up, particularly in Shanghai. There were signs of activity by foreign companies. PRC companies were accessing foreign capital through the newly established Shanghai and Shenzhen Stock Exchanges and through Hong Kong. New hotels had been built. There were cars everywhere, as well as more bicycles—and hardly any Mao suits. Three months later, in April 1994, I headed again for the Middle Kingdom, this time for a five-year stay, during which I would be responsible for developing my firm's capabilities in the PRC, focusing initially on Shanghai and Beijing.

In January 1999, some 70 years after Noel Coward put pen to paper, I began this book while staying at the newly completed Shangri-La Hotel on the east side of the Huang Pu River overlooking the Bund, in the emerging Pudong area of Shanghai. Shanghai had been reborn, yet in a different form. Foreign capital had poured into the city over the last 10 years. Foreign management and modern technology had been transferred to make up for years of neglect. The city was booming again. The Mayor of Shanghai was able to boast that you are more likely to meet the CEO of a Fortune 500 company in Shanghai than in any other city in the world.

It delights me that so many global companies that had operations in Shanghai before the Second World War, and who are major players in China today, agreed to participate in this book. Among those companies, American International Group (AIG) was actually founded in Shanghai in 1929 and has returned to the head office it once occupied, Number 17, The Bund. Bayer's first office in China was established in Shanghai in 1913. Price Waterhouse had a presence in Shanghai dating from 1903. The Asiatic Petroleum Company, a forerunner of Royal Dutch Shell, had its major office in Shanghai in The Asiatic Building, with the prestigious address of Number 1, The Bund. Otis Elevator and Carrier Air-Conditioning, now part of United Technologies Corporation, established operations in Shanghai in the first decade of this century. Why have these major global companies returned, after an absence of 40 years? What are the prospects of financial reward? How is China different from other operating environments? What are the key success factors? It is my intention, through interviews with leading foreign business leaders in China, to answer these and other questions.

I have written this book after spending five years as chairman and chief executive of Coopers & Lybrand China and, postmerger, chairman of PricewaterhouseCoopers (PwC) China. The experience has changed my outlook on life, on business, and, not least, on China. We foreigners imagine that we have much to teach the Chinese, and so we have. This is a country that has missed out on the postwar development of management science and Western technology. But China is catching up fast, and the traffic is not just one-way. One of the world's oldest civilizations also has much to teach the foreigner: the skills of listening and understanding different points of view, the arts of strategy and negotiation, the power of reconciliation and compromise, and unique perspectives on recognizing and developing competitive advantage.

Trade with China continues to grow. The PRC is the world's second-largest recipient of inbound investment, after the United States. At the time of writing, relations between China and the Western nations, particularly the United States, were turbulent. The unfortunate bombing by NATO of the Chinese Embassy in Belgrade and serious allegations of Chinese espionage in U.S. nuclear research labs were causing tension. Yet six months later, as this book was going to press, China and the United States had agreed to terms on China's accession to the World Trade Organization (WTO). There will always be interruptions in the progress of international trade and multinational business with China. Human rights issues, trade surpluses, and differences over Taiwan and Tibet can be relied upon to create unpleasantness at awkward moments. Tensions are never far below the surface. Yet the fates of China and the Western nations are becoming inextricably linked. Elyot and Amanda, the lead characters in Noel Coward's play *Private Lives,* cannot live with each other, yet they cannot live apart.

The leaders of foreign companies doing business in China must chart a course that enables them to sail safely through a changing and occasionally hostile environment. This is not an easy task. There are no obvious solutions. I trust that this book will contribute to a better understanding of the issues and to fully mutual success.

1
Reflections on China at the End of the Second Millennium

China has given much to the West. Paper, pasta, porcelain, gunpowder, azaleas, and mandarin oranges are a few of the contributions from a civilization that has lasted for over 5000 years.

Despite the flow of trade that gave rise to this transfer of everything from technology to plant species, China's borders have remained closed to foreigners for much of this time. At the end of the eighteenth century, George III of England sent an ambassador to the "Middle Kingdom" (the meaning of the Chinese words for "China") to explore the opening up of trade routes. Emperor Qianlong rebuffed him, and the encounter demonstrated a lack of willingness to accept the other's point of view or his customs. Chinese perceptions of their own historical achievements and cultural superiority were powerful forces against the need for further contact with outsiders.

In the nineteenth century, the expansionist British and French governments used force where diplomacy had failed. The Opium Wars, the sacking of the Summer Palace in Beijing, and the treaties that legalized the handing over of Hong Kong to Great Britain were, and still are, regarded with great shame by the Chinese people. As the Qing dynasty neared its end, China experienced hard times.

The foreign domination of Shanghai in the 1920s and 1930s, the Japanese invasion of China that began in 1931, and the massacre of Chinese citizens at Nanjing in 1937 increased the suspicion and fear. In the 1940s, backing of Chiang Kai-shek's Nationalist Army by the U.S. government and its allies encouraged a negative attitude toward foreigners among the victorious Communists who seized power in 1949. Borders were again closed and were to remain so for 30 years.

After three decades of social advancement amid mixed economic results, China's leaders decided in 1978 that, to develop the economy, it was necessary to reopen the country's borders. Foreign trade and investment would bring much-needed modern technology and capital. This "Opening Up," as it became known, progressed slowly but steadily during the 1980s, and halted temporarily in 1989 after the Tiananmen Incident, when many foreign companies fled the country. It resumed again in earnest after Deng Xiaoping's historic visit in March 1992 to Guangdong Province in the south of the country, neighboring Hong Kong. Although retired from office, the former paramount leader urged the Chinese people to be bolder about making reforms, and he reassured foreign investors.

The overseas Chinese from Hong Kong, Taiwan, and Singapore were the first to appreciate the significance of this visit. It confirmed in their minds that China wanted to become part of the world economy, and they seized the business opportunity presented by the Chinese government's new policies. Capital poured in to construct new offices, expatriate residential accommodation, and factories, particularly in 1992 and 1993.

Then the world's major corporations began to recognize the potential offered by China's huge market and large pool of low-cost labor. A gold rush mentality gripped many global corporate headquarters. Head office management believed that it was important to secure a presence, a foothold in this evolving economy, before the competition gained an advantage. Morgan Stanley's analyst, Barton Biggs, famously said that he was "maximum bullish" about China. Foreign bankers were eager to lend. Time was of the essence. This fever was accompanied by huge increases in GDP in China, which topped 14 percent in 1992, and which in turn led to consumer price inflation of 24 percent in 1994.

From 1995, the PRC government began to reduce the rate of inflation by slowing growth and redirected investment into productive ventures. Capital flows into property began to tail off, while the huge injection of money, management, and know-how by multinational corporations into business ventures increased. Even when the East Asian economic crisis occurred in 1997, inward investment into China continued. China had become, after the United States, the second-largest recipient of foreign direct investment in the world. Meanwhile, China's exports increased and its trade surplus grew to US$40 billion annually. The standard of living increased each year, as the Chinese people enjoyed the newfound prosperity created by economic liberalization. The new Socialist Market Economy was bringing economic benefits that the previous generation had not imagined, much less experienced.

During the second half of the 1990s, the initial enthusiasm and euphoria on the part of global companies gave way to greater realism. It became clear that this was not an easy country in which to do business. The regulatory environment was tough. Laws and regulations kept changing and were interpreted in various ways in different parts of the country. In the early years, foreign companies had chosen or had been directed by ministries or local governments toward Chinese joint venture partners; many of these turned out to be less than satisfactory as business associates. Their dissimilar objectives and their shortcomings had not been so obvious at the time agreements were negotiated. This was especially so where joint venture contracts were negotiated quickly and the resulting partnership was later to fall far short of the "contracted" expectations of both parties. There had been the pressure to catch the market—or perhaps to enhance the global chairman's first visit to China for an audience with a minister at the Diaoyutai State Guest House in Beijing.

Now the cracks were beginning to appear. Distribution systems in China were worse than anticipated, while government regulations prevented foreigners from establishing their own distribution capabilities. Quality components and raw materials proved more difficult to source than joint venture partners had represented. Chinese partners entrusted with core functions such as sales and marketing, human resource development, even government relations, fell short of the foreign investors' expectations of performance. The list of problems and complaints was endless. As a result, the start-up period for joint ventures took longer than budgeted in business plans. Projected profits were taking longer to materialize. Many companies found they had invested resources far ahead of the actual market opportunity. The rate of investment outpaced the rate of return.

It was not that these problems were absent in 1993, 1994, and 1995, and then suddenly emerged in 1996. "It was," in the words of Jack Perkowski of Asimco, "more the case that if a company had a problem in the early days, when the press was bullish about China, management was unlikely to talk about it, since this would point to something wrong with your company, or your strategy, or the way you were doing business." By the late 1990s, negative investment sentiment, fueled by the nagging persistence of both trade and non-trade issues separating China from the more mature economies, coincided with a new frugality imposed by many global headquarters on their China operations.

Then, in early 1999, the PRC government permitted the state-sponsored Guangdong International Trust and Investment Corporation (GITIC) to go into liquidation. Perceived to be backed by the state, the failure of this enterprise, which had received huge foreign loans, marked a watershed in the confidence of foreign bankers. The collapse, in the late 1990s, in equity prices of PRC enterprises whose shares were owned by foreign institutions also caused foreign fund managers to shy away from the market. The flow of initial public offerings (IPOs) of PRC corporate shares all but dried up, with little immediate prospect of recovery.

Global companies began investing on a large scale in China in 1993. Senior executives have therefore had six or seven years' experience of operating seriously in the country. The views of the 11 chairmen interviewed for this book collectively reflect more than 120 man-years of hands-on experience of managing businesses in Asia. These individuals are collectively responsible for over 160 legal entities doing business in China.

Based on their views and on the experience of Pricewaterhouse Coopers in China, what issues have foreign companies faced during the 1990s, and what lessons have been learned?

Lessons Learned

The Market

China is not one uniform, integrated market, but many. In many respects, China resembles Europe. Geographically, linguistically, culturally, and economically, it is very diverse. Because communications in the country have been so poor for so long, it made sense for each province to have its own supplies of almost all products and services. Given the size and complexity of China, the provinces were often left to marshal their own resources as best they could. The arrangements for governing the country also created different markets. Major cities such as Beijing, Chongqing, Shanghai, and Tianjin were created as administrative regions, including large areas of neighboring agricultural land. The thinking was that this would at least give the city control over the food supply for its urban population.

China today is not a market of 1.3 billion people. This misconception misled some foreign investors, at least initially. Living standards and consumer purchasing power on the east coast of China (Guangdong Province, Fujien Province, Zhejiang Province, Jiangsu

Province, and around Shanghai) are more than 5 to 10 times the level of the poorer west and south of the country and of the north. In the latter areas, export-focused activities are fewer, and restructuring of state-owned enterprises is a priority. The market for lower-priced consumer goods may be large, but for some higher-priced products such as automobiles the market is in many respects similar in size to that of one of the smaller European countries.

The Chinese market is fast-changing and difficult to read. It is also being constrained, in ways that have not previously been fully appreciated, by space, energy and environmental considerations.

In the words of Brian Anderson of Shell, "The biggest problem I have is getting a handle on the marketplace. Matching our investment in China to the growth in the market is a tricky game. Normally, in a new market, we would import our products and test the market out first. If the circumstances and the financial projections looked right, we would then invest and build capacity. Here in China, that's not possible. You have to invest up front—and that's a killer."

In most industries in China, the shape of the market is changing. Timing is crucial. For example, consider cellular phones. Ten years ago they hardly existed in China, while at the beginning of 1999, there were over 25 million cell phones, and the cellular market is growing exponentially. Every three years the number of fixed-line phones is doubling. Household appliances and entertainment electronics, virtually unknown a decade ago, are now found in 70 to 80 percent of China's homes.

By contrast, development of the automotive market has been slower than expected. In 1995, passenger car sales were projected to be 1 million units by 2001. Recent projections have been downgraded to less than 500,000. Existing capacity in China to manufacture passenger cars is more than twice the market demand.

In the health care sector, traditional Chinese medicines (known as TCMs for short) have a tremendous following, especially for the cost-effective treatment of chronic illnesses. Where Western medicines have gained a foothold (for example in the treatment of acute infectious diseases), foreign pharmaceuticals companies find themselves competing with state-owned enterprises and struggling to protect their intellectual property. And it remains unclear how medicines that have stood the test of 1000 years will blend in with or be replaced by Western medicines, which are becoming increasingly fashionable in China. Conversely, it should of course be mentioned that TCMs are becoming increasingly popular and fashionable in the West as a means of providing a softer treatment for chronic ailments.

Competition

The Chinese, like the Japanese before them, excel at copying Western products and adapting them where necessary for the local environment. Similar but typically lower-quality products are offered at lower prices by lower-cost domestic producers. Many foreign companies, particularly in consumer products, have large legal departments in China devoted to searching out counterfeit goods and to protecting their intellectual property rights. However, legal judgments against infringements can take longer than in other countries and enforcement, especially at a local level, has been extremely uneven.

If the local competition is fierce, that from other foreign companies is even fiercer. As Bruno Lemagne of Unilever puts it, "Today, in Europe, you have European, some American, and a few Japanese competitors. In Japan, you have Japanese, some American, and a few European competitors. In the United States, you have American, some European, and a few Japanese competitors. But in China, everyone is here. The competitive pressure will not go away. Competition will stay. It does not frighten us. However, it doesn't make life easy."

At the time of writing, the problem is that in many industries in China there is massive overcapacity. Whether it be automotive, consumer products, electricity generation, electronics, or new technology, too much was invested in the 1990s. Many foreign investors were so focused on overcoming the regulatory hurdles to gain market entry that, in hindsight, projects did not always meet normal commercial criteria. Coupled with this, the growth in GDP slowed in 1997 and 1998, partly as a deliberate strategy to contain inflation and partly as a result of the East Asian economic crisis. A new level of uncertainty began to influence consumer behavior in the PRC. Savings rates continued at high levels, while willingness to spend on consumer products declined abruptly. Consumer surveys showed a shift toward longer-term savings goals—housing, old-age health care, and higher education for children and grandchildren.

As a consequence, consumer demand within China faltered in 1998 and 1999 and, except for a few industries, competition proved to be so fierce that prices actually fell. Despite this, a study in April 1999 by *China Economic News* showed that of the top 500 foreign-invested enterprises, only 47 were loss-making. This statistic, which surprised many China watchers, was borne out by the experience of PricewaterhouseCoopers clients in the PRC. Perhaps things were not so bad after all for the foreign investor.

The Regulatory Environment

Control is a dominant feature of Chinese society. Scholars of Chinese history have characterized this as a feature of a "hydraulic society," where large-scale public works coupled with efficient coordination of individual activity are required for basic survival. For example, in a village, ensuring the right quantity and flow of water to each field at successive levels on a hillside is a prerequisite for growing rice productively. Thus, control of the water supply is in the interest of the entire community. In such a situation, it is natural for the village council (or at a national level, the central planners) to provide guidance, incentives, and controls.

Approvals and licenses are required for anything and everything. For the Chinese, to secure employment in a different part of the country may be difficult because approval is required. Obtaining a passport to travel abroad, particularly to Hong Kong Special Administrative Region (SAR), takes a long time. To marry or have children requires permission from the work unit. This is a Chinese phenomenon, developed over centuries by successive generations of mandarins anxious to ensure that the Emperor's decrees and the wishes of the court in Beijing were obeyed by subjects many thousands of miles away.

Hard experience over the last 50 years, including the famines of the Great Leap Forward in the 1950s and the trauma of the Cultural Revolution in the late 1960s and 1970s, has made the Chinese leadership extremely concerned about consensus and stability. Even with the introduction of greater rights of private ownership, the Party and the Government will still wish to support the socially and economically deprived.

The Chinese leaders have witnessed what can happen when change is allowed to occur too quickly and with inadequate control. They will not permit the horrors experienced in Russia in recent years to be repeated in the PRC. With 1.3 billion people to care for, the risks are too great. Control is essential to stability. As Hank Greenberg of AIG explains, "The thing that China cannot tolerate is chaos. Chaos would destroy China. To create political instability in a country with that mass of population, until there is further progress and maturity in a political and social sense, would be quite wrong. Change will come. But it will come in China's time, not on or of a timetable of external forces." Control permits gradual change, a value that is both Asian and Chinese. For Western companies used to getting things done quickly in a less regulated environment, these strictures seem burdensome and are certainly time-consuming. They are also contrary to the invisible hand of market forces venerated by foreign investors for whom Adam Smith is a more familiar sage than Confucius.

A further aggravation is caused by the fact that the rules seem to be forever changing and are capable of being variously interpreted by different officials in different provinces. As the country's economy evolves from one that is centrally planned and state-owned to one where market forces operate and diverse means of ownership are permitted, the laws and regulations need to be changed. There is no precise model to follow. Thus, if a policy and its accompanying regulations do not appear to work, the law is changed.

Such changes occur frequently. Further, Chinese regulations have for centuries been interpreted by local officials on the basis of loosely worded legislation. Scholars of Chinese law point out that in China rules and regulations are administrative rather than judicial in nature. Most significant developments in economic law and regulation are preceded by years of experimentation. Written legal guidance is codified only after contending views have been reconciled and senior officials are satisfied that they are favorable to the State's interests.

The vagaries of the process and the uncertainty of regulations are aggravated by the complex and incomplete reforms of the judiciary itself. In the first three decades of the PRC's existence, the courts were, in the opinion of many commentators, instruments of the political leadership. Few serious economic cases were ever adjudicated according to any explicit commercial law. The existing contract law was developed in the mid-1980s, although the courts had little experience in enforcing it before the early 1990s. Contract law is, therefore, in its early stages of development. Having said this, I should also make clear that efforts are being made by the State Council and the People's Congress to invoke rule by law rather than rule by man, although this requires a radical change in generations of habitual practice.

The gradual "Opening Up" of China's market has not been as speedy in certain industries, such as financial services, as it has in others, such as consumer products. This has caused frustration to foreign companies and delays in licenses being granted to undertake business. It took AIG 17 years of patient relationship building and contributions to China to obtain the first license to be issued to a foreign insurer, in 1992.

The numerous licenses and approvals required from different authorities when the door has been opened can prove exasperating. In a recent review by a newly appointed PRC official, no fewer than 27 licenses were found to be necessary to operate a multidisciplinary accountancy and consultancy practice; in the UK, a maximum of just three would have sufficed. These burdensome requirements are not only numerous, they are also fragmentary and poorly coordinated. Ministers and senior officials do not oversee a coordinated system of licensing and regulation. Rather, they manage numerous bureaucracies that struggle for revenue and power through licenses, fees, and taxes that they individually create and promote.

Apart from being overlicensed, China is also overregulated. But these are inescapable features of doing business in China, where the simplest of tasks can take three times as long as elsewhere. Happily, looking forward, these deterrents to effective business have not escaped the notice of the more reform-minded ministers and officials, who are determined to make China's economy more efficient. But this will take time, and China needs time—a theme that commentators have repeated over the centuries.

The Importance of Government

In China, where the environment is heavily regulated and where public ownership has been the basis of production for so long, government has a far greater impact on business activities than in many other countries. Of course, in agrochemicals, energy, pharmaceuticals, and telecommunications, central government is never far away in any country because of the importance of these industries to the welfare of society. In China, the historical influence of ideology is mixed with concerns over security and control.

As Terry Barnett of Novartis explains, with its horrendous famines in the 1930s and, after the Revolution, during the Great Leap Forward, China's leaders are obsessed with the objective of self-sufficiency in food. China wants the security of having all its agricultural products and inputs grown or made in China. This has led to the encouragement in agrochemicals of synthesis plants, to make the basic substance that is then formulated into the final product.

The commitment to self-sufficiency was not limited to the agricultural sector. Much of the collectivization and communization of all productive units in the Maoist era was focused on creating micro self-sufficient economies. As one of the basic ideologies of that era, this created movements that promoted everything from family pig farming to family pig-iron furnaces. At the other extreme from this pervasive subscale inefficiency was the superscale inefficiency of the massive state-run industrial plants. Neither group was subjected to any measure of market discipline. These protected twin monuments of China's Maoist past became the twin targets of Deng Xiaoping's economic reforms.

The importance of government in China is something that all successful foreign investors must recognize and accommodate. For U.S. companies, as Randy Yeh of Lucent advises, "a sound, stable and good relationship between the United States and the PRC is key to business success in China." Given the growing trade imbalance with the United States and the views of Congress on such subjects as human rights, Taiwan, and Tibet, the going is unlikely to be smooth. The impact of politics on the business prospects of American companies can be significant. Some British companies believed they were disadvantaged in securing contracts in China as a result of the "Cold War" climate that prevailed prior to the handing back of Hong Kong in 1997. To counter these political influences, the senior executives of global companies in China spend a significant part of their time nurturing relations with government ministers and regulatory agencies, both in Beijing and at the provincial and municipal levels.

For Shell, China is no different in this respect from other countries. As Brian Anderson puts it, "If we can develop the right relationship, then we can have frank and open dialogue." The importance of good relations with government in China cannot be overemphasized. When Zhu Rongji was the Mayor of Shanghai, Hank Greenberg helped him establish Shanghai's first international business advisory council, a prestigious annual gathering that the chairmen of many global companies aspire to join. This and other expressions of goodwill are necessary in order to build the relationship and demonstrate that your company is a true "friend of China." Such favors tend to be repaid in the form of licenses and contracts.

The Importance of Relationships

In China, one of the first words a foreigner learns is *guanxi*, which means *connections* or *relationships*. This is the process by which each side seeks to establish who the other is, whom the other knows, and whether they are respectively able to deliver what each promises.

Anywhere in the world, networking and building relationships are important to business success. As Richard Latham of United Technologies reflects, "People come to China and think that they have stumbled across something that is so entirely unique that only the Chinese are concerned with it. What is different about China is the sort of intensive preoccupation with relationship building that goes on—the whole time. It's an almost consuming aspect of Chinese life. Foreign managers fail to realize how pervasive it is and that, at every meeting, social or business, the other partner is working on some aspect of the relationship." While the process of relationship building is not peculiar to China, it does take longer than elsewhere because of the lack of information about people and organizations and because of the complexities of the society. The weak legal environment and the lack of transparency mean that many objectives can only be achieved through *guanxi*.

All too often in China, one hears that a foreign company has a poor relationship with its joint venture partner, or that another multinational corporation has been able to obtain a license because of its excellent relationships with ministers and officials.

The concept of mutual back-scratching (but certainly not bribery) is essential to success. While it is not necessary or at all desirable to present lavish gifts or to transfer funds to numbered bank accounts, to achieve one's objectives it is important to be helpful. Many foreign companies spend huge sums on training programs and overseas educational visits for PRC officials and leaders of state enterprises in order to demonstrate commitment and to build relationships with regulators and potential joint venture partners.

It is sometimes difficult for management back home to appreciate that its on-site managers must spend what appears to be an inordinate amount of time in building and maintaining such relationships.

Closely linked to relationships is the issue of "face." In a society that has a weak legal system, consensus is important. Frequently, a problem can only be solved if one party backs down. Those who back down today may be those who see others back down tomorrow. Face needs to be preserved. If not, relationships can break down and will be difficult, if not impossible, to reestablish.

The Shortage of Qualified Management

It should come as no surprise that in China there is not a large pool of managerial talent trained to international standards. For 30 years, the economic system was based on central planning; state ownership of the means of production; absence of a market; and directives given to production units concerning what to make, when to make it, where to send it, and at what price to sell it. Time was definitely not money. There was no local competition and foreign companies were not permitted to trade. The managers of business enterprises were administrators carrying out orders, who had little or no experience operating in a competitive market environment. Yet subsequent to the Opening Up in 1978, Deng Xiaoping encouraged the Chinese to be more entrepreneurial, and many rose to the occasion with great success.

In this environment, there are twin problems: managers whose behavior is entirely bureaucratic, shaped by decades of compliance; and managers who are wildly entrepreneurial, fueled by decades of frustration and evasion. As Jack Perkowski graphically points out, "If the management you have in China is too bureaucratic, you can't get anything done. On the other hand, if it is at the other end of the spectrum, you can't sleep at night because these cowboy entrepreneurs practice a brand of management that no multinational company would feel comfortable with. You might be in the components business today and find that you are in the hotel business tomorrow."

When global companies began to establish businesses in China during the 1980s, and to a greater extent in the 1990s, there was no available managerial talent trained in Western methods. Senior executives had to be shipped in from abroad, together with their personal effects, which often included the fridge, the lawn mower, and the family pet. The cost of expatriate housing was kept artificially high by a shortage of supply. The "hardship" premiums, together with allowances for children's education and medical care, added to mounting payroll costs. It was an expensive business.

A further problem was the steep learning curve for those expatriates who did not have previous experience of Asia and who did not speak Mandarin. It takes time to understand China. The culture is very strong. The civilization is perhaps the oldest remaining in the world. Language and literature, idioms and nuances of meaning are as complex as you will find in any country. Failure to take the time to understand can result in costly mistakes by well-meaning but ill-informed expatriate executives.

The Problem with Joint Venture Partners

A joint venture will survive for as long as the objectives of the parties to the joint venture remain compatible. All too often, the Chinese partner has different objectives from the foreign partner, and these are not always identified when the joint venture is formed. Kent Watson considers that the difference in expectations is often the biggest barrier to success. He comments, "Foreign investors in China hope for a financial return on the investments they make. They seek a return, perhaps over a long time frame, from access to the large market and from the lower cost of labor. On the other hand, Chinese joint venture partners want technology and know-how, together with capital and modern equipment, and they invariably expect dividends immediately."

Any gap in initial expectations is exacerbated by changing expectations in the early years of a joint venture. Once technology is successfully assimilated into a joint venture, Chinese partners resent having to pay for it in perpetuity either through a technical service fee or through the equity presence of the foreign partner. On the other hand, once the initial regulatory and licensing processes are complete, foreign partners soon resent how little the Chinese partner is able to contribute to the basic business needs of the venture—for example, marketing, distribution, and management development.

The relationships between Chinese and foreign partners are not helped by the baggage of history, which tends to create barriers between the two parties. The Chinese people's underlying mistrust of foreigners, coupled with the sense of cultural superiority and the desire no longer to be treated as the underdog, results in tensions that are sometimes hard to defuse. And the prosperity that foreigners display in China makes many Chinese feel that they have a right to a slice of that wealth.

A further problem is that the expatriate assigned to make the joint venture work often is not the same expatriate who negotiated the deal. The Chinese place great value on personal relationships built up during the course of negotiations. Trust and confidence are developed through a frank exchange of views. However, views expressed and verbal promises made when the joint venture is being constructed may not always be reflected in the legal contracts and are all too often forgotten later, especially if foreign management changes continually. The failure to agree on objectives and to understand the other side's point of view is amusingly captured in the Chinese expression "to share the same bed but to have different dreams."

Problems have also been created by the PRC government's desire to transfer technology and know-how to state-owned enterprises selected as potential partners based on political objectives or cronyism rather than on sound economic reasons. Chinese partners who purport to have access to distribution systems or reliable sources of raw materials or components have too often been found, in practice, to be sadly lacking. The disappointment experienced by international companies is reflected in the increasing desire to liquidate joint ventures and change them into wholly foreign-owned enterprises ("WFOEs," or "wooffies," as they are known).

In practice in the longer term, a joint venture has been rarely found, anywhere in the world, to be an ideal vehicle for business success. In China, it is used as a method of transferring foreign technology and know-how while retaining an element of Chinese control. It is hardly surprising, then, that so many joint ventures are considered to have failed. But there are some highly successful ones and these are, of course, much publicized.

Communication with the Head Office

The incidence of failure among expatriate senior executives in China is very high. According to some studies, the failure rate is twice the world average. How is it that highfliers with 20 years of experience in a company can so often fail when they are sent to China? The problems of harmonizing the expectations imposed by two contrasting business cultures cannot be overemphasized. As Kent Watson explains, "On the one hand you have the demands of the home office corporate management, who probably negotiated an agreement that they were sure would succeed. On the other hand, you have the Chinese manager and the people who negotiated the agreement for the Chinese side, who are also looking to you to make the venture successful. Then you have the poor expatriate manager who has been seconded to China to make the whole thing work. He is in a lose/lose scenario."

Too often, the board member responsible for China back home changes. Each time there is a change, there is a chance that corporate strategy might change, and there is typically an interval of time before the new senior executive gets up to speed in understanding China. The burden of educating head office management usually falls on the top managers in China, who are then often cast in an advocacy role for projects they did not create. When profits take longer to materialize and the forecasts in the business plan are not met, it is easy to forget the peculiarities of the Chinese operating environment. Criticism can come too swiftly.

Michael Portoff of Bayer has a view on this: "The picture is very complex in this country. Therefore, you have to paint a realistic picture to your board of management. You must not conceal or withhold the difficulties, the problems, and the challenges. This is not a champagne-drinking country. It is still a place for the pioneer. You have to roll your sleeves up. In our presentations at Bayer's head office, we have referred to China as a 'giant with certain weaknesses.' It is not an Eldorado, nor is it a country with no hope. If this is how you describe it, then people will not have unrealistic expectations. In addition, you absolutely need the backing of your board of management at home and of the executives at headquarters. Otherwise you cannot work in these difficult and complex surroundings."

Solutions

Much has been written recently about the difficulties of doing business in China and on the disillusionment developing in global boardrooms. Toward the end of 1998, the PRC authorities became concerned about declining levels of foreign direct investment and sought to reverse the trend. Mayors and foreign investment commissioners from a number of cities met with intermediary organizations, requesting assistance to encourage further inbound investment. It has been suggested that the drive for WTO accession by the premier, Zhu Rongji, was partly influenced by China's desire to maintain the interest of global companies.

While foreign technology and capital poured into China during the 1990s and stimulated the protected domestic economy, US$300 billion of inbound investment is not enough. China is a big country, and its appetite for capital is bigger still. A great deal of the investment to date emanated from overseas Chinese who ploughed it into small-scale businesses and real estate. In the last 10 years, over 85 percent of China's fixed asset and infrastructure investment has been funded from domestic capital sources. However, strains in the state banking system and the lessons of the East Asian crisis have influenced China's leaders to seek more foreign capital in the form of direct investment. The Opening Up to foreign companies must continue in order to maintain the growth in GDP that the country needs to transform its economy.

While the issues facing multinational companies will become easier to handle with the passage of time, the lessons learned over the last 10 years will continue to be relevant for executives in the first decade of the new millennium. It is both tempting and dangerous to try to draw a road map of how to succeed in China. Every industry, every company, and every situation is different and requires individual attention. With change taking place in China at a dizzying pace, in the time it takes to publish this book much of the terrain will have shifted. However, some of the essential features of success can be described.

Research and Due Diligence

It seems almost too obvious to mention, but too little time is spent by corporate executives on researching the market in China and analyzing business opportunities. As Richard Latham observes, "When I listen to managers from all sorts of companies, I'm often surprised at how nebulous their goals and objectives are before they come to China. They form partnerships and they can't figure out why they did it. Probably the truth of the matter is they didn't give much thought to it in the beginning. They didn't do their homework. You know, it's amazing that many times companies don't know what questions to ask. The Chinese will answer precisely the questions they are asked. But they usually won't volunteer answers to fill in the gaps and they won't think about the questions the foreigner didn't ask. They take the view that the foreigner must know what he is doing."

Richard Latham's comments suggest that there is a certain irony in the way that improved knowledge about doing business in China derails a reasonable entry process. Executives know that negotiating projects can take an inordinately long time. This prompts them to measure success more by how quickly they can get through the negotiation process and less by how skillfully they conduct the negotiations and how good a foundation they create for the business. Executives know that a labyrinth of regulatory problems lies ahead of them in the entry process. This prompts them to focus resources more on navigating through that labyrinth than on developing a reliable market model and investment plan. Executives know that their Chinese partners are masters of *guanxi* and that the more important they are, the better their *guanxi*. This prompts them to overestimate the impact of the Chinese partners' relationships on the ultimate success of the business and to rely excessively on their partners to resolve problems of compliance that should have been identified and avoided in the first place.

Based on our experience in helping multinational corporations establish operations, enter into joint ventures, and acquire businesses in China, we know that certain common issues recur. The range of problems identified during strategic planning, negotiations, and due diligence assignments is best illustrated by a long list:

- Misunderstanding of the market
- Quality of the management
- Bureaucratic hurdles
- Distribution difficulties
- Quality of production
- Supply of components
- Unwanted employees and social liabilities
- Title to property
- Reliability of accounting records
- Misstatement of inventory and receivables
- Misstatement of liabilities
- Valuation of fixed assets
- Quality of systems
- Quality of finance staff

If you establish operations in China but don't encounter and address most of these issues at the beginning, before the commitment is made, then it is probable that at a later date you will be in for a rude shock.

Choice of Partner

With further relaxation encouraged by WTO negotiations—even accession—and the growing confidence of the Chinese authorities, in many industries a joint venture will still remain the only available route to market entry for many years to come. On the positive side, the PRC government is gradually taking a less prescriptive approach to the choice of joint venture partner. In the early stages of the Opening Up, there was greater governmental direction. Except in sensitive industries, the foreigner is increasingly being allowed more freedom to choose, based on business rather than political or macroeconomic considerations. With increased choice comes the need for greater care to identify precisely what might be expected of a joint venture partner and to confirm that what is expected can be delivered.

"Don't rush," is the advice given by foreign executives who have negotiated and operated joint ventures. Jim Conybeare of John Swire & Sons has established no fewer than 21 joint ventures in China involving some of the world's leading companies. One of his most successful joint ventures is the Coca-Cola franchise in Guangdong Province. "That took three years to negotiate," he notes, "and, after all that time, we got to know each other pretty well. As a result, we have an excellent relationship at board level."

Another common piece of advice is the need for alternatives when negotiating a joint venture. The Chinese side understands the concept of competition and may seek to play one foreign company off against another. It is not out of order for the foreigner to adopt the same tactic. After all, it is in the interest of both parties to ensure that, going forward, they have the right partner.

"Don't put all your eggs in one basket," is another maxim offered by a number of chairmen. For example, granting a national pan-China franchise to one joint venture could prove to be a costly mistake if the partnership does not work out. Sometimes, it is preferable to limit the joint venture's geographical scope to a single city or province. Retaining flexibility is crucial.

The Right Approach to the Market

"It's not one market but many," is the observation made repeatedly by the chairmen interviewed for this book. "It's changing so fast," is another. There is little doubt that with personal incomes in China increasing annually at a rate of over 10 percent, the market for goods and services of all types is expanding. What makes China more complicated than other markets is the continued interaction of government and business.

Bruno Lemagne believes that China differs from other countries with regard to the specifics of consumer products, but that the strategic issues are the same. In his view, the key to business success is adaptation. "Wall's ice cream is well-known in many countries, but its flavors vary region by region, based on local taste and local culinary history. In the West, for example, people like their ice cream to contain a lot of dairy and a lot of sugar. Not so in China, where neither features in the Chinese diet. Tastes are different. It is more likely then that the next ice cream flavor in China will not be mint chocolate chip or tiramisu, but red bean."

Similar considerations apply to communicating with customers. The content and style of advertisements vary within Europe from one country to another. In China, the messages and the way they are communicated have to be tailored to the specific audience being targeted. For Terry Barnett, the answer to these uncertainties is to get closer to the market—not just in the big cities but in the rural areas as well. As he stresses, "It is necessary to understand the customer mentality and the way it is changing."

Expatriate Management

There is an emerging view that the chances of success are greatly enhanced if senior executives sent to China have knowledge and experience of Asia and also have Chinese language capabilities. In

Asia, "relationships" and "face" assume added importance. "Look at 'loss of face,' " reflects Bruno Lemagne. "Are there many people who would like to lose face? This is not particularly a Chinese issue. However, the way it is dealt with, the way it is interpreted, is very Chinese." These matters take time to understand, as do the different methods of communicating. Richard Latham explains, "To begin to understand how to operate in China, it helps you to understand the differences between Chinese society and its people and the society and people you know back home. There is a Chinese way of looking at things and a Chinese way of doing things." On the question of language, he advises that "you can get by using English, but you may be missing 60 percent of what is going on."

In an environment where everything can seem hostile—culture, regulators, joint venture partners—alienation can set in quite easily, particularly if head office support begins to wane. Multinational corporations need to consider carefully the qualities that are necessary in executives they select for secondment to China. Character defects and skill deficiencies can be magnified when managers are put under pressure in these unfamiliar surroundings.

Successful expatriates must be persistent, patient, and flexible. As Jack Perkowski puts it, the ideal candidate is "someone who does not take no for an answer, someone who is willing to roll up his sleeves, someone with the relevant experience who will do things he probably hasn't done for 10 or 15 years." Kent Watson goes further, adding that "people who have an interest in the language, people who are sensitive to cultural differences, people who get beyond their expatriate world, are far more effective in accomplishing what needs to be done."

The reality is that China has much to teach the foreigner. It is not just a one-way transfer of technology and know-how. The foreigner who listens, learns, and adapts is more likely to be successful.

Localization

Localization has been described as "the coin of the realm" or "like motherhood and apple pie." Certainly, everyone is doing it. The

PRC government encourages localization, in part based on a deeply held view that the Chinese do not want the foreigner to control, ever again, their economy and businesses. Xenophobia is a phenomenon found in most countries, but in China there is perhaps more historical justification for such an attitude. There is also a natural desire that the Chinese people rather than others be the first to enjoy the benefits of economic progress in their own country. These are understandable sentiments.

Regardless of the governmental objective, localization is a key priority for every multinational corporation operating in the country. This is important not only because it reduces the significant cost of expatriates, but because it provides a career progression for Chinese employees. Randy Yeh of Lucent, for example, notes that "We have established training and career development plans for all employees to demonstrate to our people that we are serious and that we have their long-term interest at heart."

Jim Conybeare had no fewer than 1200 indigenous salesmen attending the Swire Group's sales training program in the first quarter of 1999. "One of the pieces of advice I would give a potential successor," he says, "is the importance of training." Hank Greenberg ascribes an important feature in AIG's success in China to the relentless program of training, so that the business is run by Chinese and not by foreigners.

One of the most professional training programs in China has been put together by Johnson & Johnson, renowned globally for the group's focus on people development. "Outward bound" style, off-site courses seek to identify those recruits who have the potential to adapt to the international culture of a foreign company. The architect of the program, Jerry Norskog of Johnson & Johnson, explains: "When I interview a new recruit, I ask him what advice his father and mother gave him about being successful in life. The answer is usually: 'Keep your head down, keep your mouth shut, ensure you have a good relationship with your boss, be obedient, and work hard.' Now I am going to ask him to stand up, to speak out heretical ideas, to fight intellectually, to challenge his boss. I am going to tell him that risk taking is rewarded, not punished. I am literally going to turn the tables on him. He is going to have to make a 180-degree turn if he is to meet my expectations."

During the last five years, PricewaterhouseCoopers China has recruited more than 1500 PRC nationals from universities and trained them in China to become qualified accountants or consultants. It has also seconded abroad over 100 people for periods exceeding one year. Kent Watson comments, "This program is working well, but you can't rush it. You know, in any country, it takes a minimum of 10 years to take a new graduate and develop him or her into a partner. We haven't been at it that long in China."

Developing a Culture of Change

Creating and sustaining a culture of change in global companies is considered essential to corporate success. Chairmen of technology companies, such as Jorma Ollila of Nokia, put this high on their list of objectives. In China, the challenge is greater because of the country's history. If Chinese managers come from a state enterprise, there is tremendous loyalty to the old ways of doing things.

The formal training course is one way to crack the problem. Jerry Norskog points out that "the talented youngsters who are the fine products of these fine universities are also the sons and daughters of the Communist past. They have grown up in work units. Their reference point is the 'iron rice bowl.' They learn by rote, they write it all down and memorize it, and then regurgitate what they have learned when asked a question. They are very good at memorizing data and at assimilating facts and ideas, but they have not been trained to be free thinkers."

What is taught in the training course needs to be repeated and emphasized in the operating environment. Jack Perkowski explains one of the problems: "Most people, including the Chinese, don't like change. The response from a PRC general manager sometimes goes like this. 'Yes, those techniques and those practices may work in Europe and the United States. But this is China. And China is different.' They may actually believe that. Years of unfortunate contact with the foreigner have taught the Chinese that they are special. We agree that the Chinese are special. Everyone is special. But, we don't subscribe to the notion that because it works elsewhere it won't work in China. We think that, when you boil everything down, China actually operates in the same way as other places. The laws of economics apply here as they do in every part of the world. However, the fact that Chinese managers are able to argue in this way gives them an immediate excuse for not changing."

It is difficult for foreigners to change the Chinese way of doing things. There is, on occasion, a genuine and understandable mistrust of foreigners. The Chinese partners to a Sino-foreign joint venture want to control the workforce, which is the traditional manner in which Chinese organizations are controlled. There is often a fear that the foreign company will seek to cut the large workforce, and the Chinese managers do not want to abrogate their responsibility. This can lead to the retention of old-fashioned work practices.

Further, as Richard Latham notes, "We can bring into a joint venture factory a technology model of how to produce something. Our Chinese partners will try very carefully to copy the model exactly. But it will be an analogue copy, because they will have looked at it with eyes that are accustomed to seeing the analogue nature of the technology. They will miss the detail and may not understand why things are done in a certain way." In his view, the key is successfully integrating Chinese culture and Western technology. "The message is the medium," he remarks. "In our joint ventures, where we've taken the external message and wrapped it in Chinese paper, we've succeeded very well in changing ideas and work habits." You have to do it in a Chinese way, but without for one moment forgetting the objective you are striving to achieve.

Building Trust

There is general agreement that, after a history of 150 to 200 years of unfortunate contact with the foreigner, the Chinese have some reservations. The foreigner has a wall to climb if he or she is to develop trust. This task is often not helped by the very different objectives and perceptions of the two parties. Most multinational companies think and operate globally, whereas the Chinese are more nationalistic.

In the view of Michael Portoff, "Regardless of our ownership percentage, we have tried to treat our joint venture partners as equals. Trust has to be built up over a period of time. You can only achieve this if you do it in an open, honest, and frank way. During joint venture negotiations, potential problems have to be discussed at the outset rather than being left until the joint venture is founded and then the trouble begins. When you form and operate a joint venture, the emphasis has to be on the word 'joint.' You have to understand that there are different points of view. But this doesn't mean that you have to give in. To succeed, you have to get the balance right."

These sentiments are repeated by Brian Anderson: "When you are dealing with people, you can be very frank and very direct. But for it to work, they have to believe that you are sincere, and to achieve this you have to develop a good, but simple, relationship." You have to explain, very frankly, that attendance at a week-long training course will not automatically transform someone from being a state enterprise manager into an international executive. There is a tendency among some Chinese managers and officials to underestimate how long it takes and how much work is involved to reach international standards.

Problems are invariably caused by expectations not being met. For example, foreign companies sometimes find that feasibility studies, often carried out five years ago on the basis of limited experience of the country, predicted positive performance that has taken longer in practice to materialize. When the Chinese partner discovers this, mutual trust can break down because it is typically the foreigner who prepared the business plan in the first instance.

Sometimes it is too easy to gloss over problems or to sweep them under the carpet. In China, this will rarely work, since if a problem emerges and the Chinese partner believes that it should have been anticipated or that it seems to have been hidden by the foreigner, then mistrust can be created. Actions can be misunderstood. Suspicions can be easily aroused. Motives can be frequently misinterpreted.

You also have to show the benefits of investment and of retaining rather than distributing profits. The latter is the natural inclination of the Chinese partner, who is looking for a rapid return. Jim Conybeare advises, "Of course, you must not promise a level of dividend income and then suddenly try to switch it off because you need to invest more capital."

Kent Watson focuses on what needs to be done to bridge the gap. He advises, "In my view, the gap can only be bridged when the two parties are able to build a relationship of trust. The difference in objectives needs to be understood and discussed, so that mistrust is not created when doing business." He emphasizes training and career development: "Training is not just for the purpose of increasing efficiency and production. It will also create equals. We want to develop people who will become true partners. In this way we hope to develop a relationship of trust."

Randy Yeh was born in Qingdao, on China's east coast. As he was educated both in Taiwan and in the United States, where he worked for many years, he understands equally well the Western and the Chinese approaches to these issues. He is able to offer advice from a unique position: "You will always have differences, but if you act fairly, frankly, and honestly, you can make a joint venture succeed. When there is fairness on both sides, frank discussion can happen and a relationship can be built. Understanding can be established and trust will develop. Once you have trust, many things can work in China."

Managing Costs in a Volatile but Regulated Environment

Building and sustaining a business in China requires aggressive management of a range of costs—some familiar and some not. Many businesses find themselves in a margin squeeze that becomes the main issue in business planning and execution. The squeeze is between unforeseen pressure on costs, some commercial and some regulatory, and unforeseen pressure on prices, some commercial but many regulatory. Regulatory costs include items found in other countries, such as duties and taxes, which are subject to sudden change. They also include items that are particular to China, such as forced partnering costs; inflated real estate prices in designated investment zones; extra margins paid to state-licensed importers, distributors, and retailers; and so on. Price pressures are brought about by the mandatory involvement of local pricing bureaus, forced distribution channels, and unconstrained and subsidized state-enterprise competition.

To address these issues successfully requires the senior China executive to manage the interface with the regulatory environment actively rather than treating it purely as a compliance process. Through good relationships with regulatory officials, it is possible to influence the development of regulations as well as their inter-pretation, to the benefit of the business. For example, a process of tax planning to enhance one's tax position needs to be supported by a process of relationship management with the taxing authori-ties. A business that relies on significant imported inputs needs to be supported by a function that not only monitors compliance with customs and excise regulations but aggressively manages rela-tionships with the appropriate agencies.

Making the Long-Term Commitment

In a survey carried out in the first half of 1999 among the chairmen of the top 50 PricewaterhouseCoopers clients in China, most expressed caution and commented that the operating environment in China was more complex than had been imagined a few years ago. The focus of companies was on reducing losses and on improving profitability through consolidation of legally separate joint ventures and through operational efficiencies, including a reduction in the number of expatriates. In the short term, there was a desire to generate a better return for shareholders from invest-ments already made before committing further funds. However, there were some global companies that had not yet invested significant sums in China and had committed to doing so in the near future. The overall picture indicated a reduced level of foreign direct investment from global companies, when compared to the heady days of 1994 to 1997.

But all of the 50 chairmen surveyed were optimistic about the future and stressed the importance of multinational corporations' having a long-term vision and long-term commitment when it comes to investing in China. These views have been encouraged by the belief that the Chinese leaders know what they are doing, and, although there are many serious issues to be faced, there is confidence that they are up to the job. The zeal with which the program of market reform is being pursued has given grounds for comfort, as has the desire to restructure the loss-making state enterprises and the nonperforming loans of the state banks. The decision made in early 1999 by Premier Zhu Rongji to make every effort to join the WTO encouraged MNC chairmen who recognized the opportunities that would be generated by the further Opening Up.

In March 1999, the People's Congress changed the constitution to provide a constitutional basis for the private sector. It was announced that contract law would be improved and that legal protections would be introduced for the private investor. By mid-1999, a comprehensive revision of contract law was in its final stages. At all levels, advocates of competition are emerging as major influencers, reminding one of the early 1980s when Margaret Thatcher championed the free market in the UK and rolled back the frontiers of socialism. This phenomenon, which spilled over to many countries and led to worldwide privatization on a massive scale, has even influenced the Chinese leadership. Of course, it is being introduced in China in a Chinese way, with a strong focus on caring for the people and on maintaining the achievements of socialism. For example, it is not called privatization but, euphemistically, "introducing diverse forms of ownership." The train has left the station, and China's desire to join the world's international organizations and become a truly global player implies a direction from which there will be no turning back. There will of course be false starts and hiccups along the way, but the direction is clear.

As Michael Portoff comments, "If you go to Beijing or Shanghai, you will not meet Mr. Marx or Mr. Engels or Mr. Hegel on the streets. This is a capitalistic country, more like what you would have seen in Manchester at the end of the nineteenth century."

Questions are often posed by journalists and commentators about the future political stability of the country. To address this issue effectively requires a separate political treatise. However, chairmen of multinational corporations seem to have confidence in the ability of the country's leaders to transform the economy within the present political framework. The control that the Party maintains over the people and over the changes taking place appears strong. Predictions of another Russia are not given much credence.

The often-turbulent relationship between China and other countries, particularly the United States and the UK, gives foreign businessmen cause for concern. Trade negotiations, commercial contracts, and the granting of licenses can all be influenced by a sudden deterioration in relations. For example, a meeting between a foreign prime minister and the Dalai Lama can be used by China as a lever against a company from that country if the meeting occurs in the middle of negotiating a joint venture. Alternatively, it might provide an excuse to the Chinese authorities to delay the granting of a license. The dimension of international politics makes life difficult for foreign businessmen in China. But this phenomenon also exists in other countries.

Economically, China has witnessed something of a miracle in the last decade. Economic statistics may be highly suspect, even "cooked," in the view of some observers, but real economic progress is highly visible. A visit to the Shanghai Pudong area or to an electronics factory in Guangdong evidences the success. Most foreign businessmen are confident that this will continue, albeit not at the rate experienced in the early 1990s.

The regulatory environment is seen as the greatest uncertainty for multinational corporations, and as the area of highest risk. China's accession to the WTO may start to reduce this, but compliance with commitments made will be a fearfully difficult challenge. The vagaries of the administrative environment will remain for many years, despite the political will for change.

In summary, the prospect of political stability, the scale and growth of the economy, and the professional manner in which it is being transformed give the chairmen of the world's top companies optimism and confidence in the longer term about the market in China. The regulatory environment continues to give concern and headaches. The need for flexibility on the part of multinational corporations doing business in China is paramount.

The dichotomy between long-term optimism and short-term caution, even despair, has interested writers and commentators on China for the last two centuries. Success in China depends on the industry you are in, the timing of market entry, and the many other issues referred to in this book.

I shall leave the last word to Hank Greenberg: "If you want to do business in China, you need to take the long-term view. You have to be patient. China is, after all, a 5000-year-old civilization. They don't measure time in the same way that we do in the West. You can't rush China. You have to take it step-by-step. That's the secret of success."

2

Step by Step

If you want to do business in China,
you have to take the long-term view.
You must be patient.
MAURICE R. ("HANK") GREENBERG
CHAIRMAN AND CHIEF EXECUTIVE
OFFICER, AMERICAN INTERNATIONAL
GROUP, INC.

Hank Greenberg has the stamina and gritty determination to make
things happen. As a boy in the United States, in order to play foot-
ball after school he was prepared to forgo the school bus and walk
the four and a half miles home. Later, as a 19-year-old in the Signal
Corps, he was attached to the U.S. Army Rangers and experienced
the landing at Omaha Beach on D-Day. His subsequent duty in
Korea, as commander of a Signals company and briefly as a defense
attorney attached to the War Crimes Commission, taught him the
importance of discipline, focus, and loyalty. For his service as a com-
bat commander in Korea, he was awarded the Bronze Star. The
influences on the lives of great men are the preserve of biographers.
However, whatever the causes, the result is clear: Hank Greenberg
is a legend in his time, a man who has developed and built one of
the world's largest and most successful insurance and financial services organizations.

American International Group (AIG) is a giant of a concern,
ranking 26th among all global companies in terms of market capi-

talization, which in April 1999 amounted to around $165 billion. Those fortunate enough to have invested in AIG's shares when it went public in 1969 have seen their investment grow a staggering 20 percent compound per annum over the last 30 years. In 1998, AIG's turnover amounted to US$33 billion, and the group operated from 130 countries.

Hank Greenberg joined AIG in 1960, after earning a degree from New York Law School and gaining initial insurance experience in Continental Casualty Corporation, where he became the youngest-ever vice president. After a successful reorganization of AIG's American Home Assurance, he was appointed to succeed the group's founder, C. V. Starr, as Chief Executive Officer in 1967.

Consistently described as a workaholic—tough, demanding, impatient, aggressive, inscrutable, focused, tireless, and tenacious—Greenberg does not suffer fools easily and is not known for "taking prisoners." But he is known for his loyalty to his senior executives and colleagues who have worked with him to make AIG a success. He also considers that relationships must be mutually beneficial—a belief that, together with his charm and courtesy, has endeared him to China's leaders, whom he has come to know well in the last two decades. AIG was the first foreign insurer to be granted a license to operate in the PRC, in 1992. For his personal contribution to the insurance industry in China, Hank Greenberg was made an honorary citizen of Shanghai—one of only seven foreigners to be so honored.

■ ■ ■

AIG's origins are in China and stem from the insurance agency, American Asiatic Underwriters (AAU), which was founded by Cornelius Vander Starr in Shanghai in November 1919. Noting that many Chinese lived to a venerable age and that improving living standards would increase life expectancy, Starr formed his own company, Asia Life Insurance Company, in Shanghai, to market life insurance to the indigenous Chinese population. Its most popular product was a 20-year endowment policy. By 1923, Asia Life had established a branch in Peking, under the leadership of an American, Mansfield Freeman, who had taught English and philosophy at Qinghua University. While a lecturer, Freeman had encouraged students who sought extracurricular advice to compete for an award from Asia Life for selling the most life assurance policies during their summer vacations. AAU and Asia Life grew and prospered, and in 1927 moved into a prestigious building, Number 17, The Bund, which became the group's East Asian headquarters. By the end of the 1920s, Shanghai had become the financial services center of Asia, and Starr was one of the city's great entrepreneurs.

From the early days, Starr's attitude toward the Chinese differed markedly from that of his fellow expatriates in Shanghai. He believed that the future lay in the hands of the indigenous people. Accordingly, he recruited bright and talented local people and developed them into managers—a practice that has remained a backbone of AIG's business philosophy. One of these recruits, K.K. Tse, who later became Chief Operating Officer in Shanghai, has reflected on his time with Starr: "Our desks faced each other for years. We worked closely together, not only in the office, but often during quiet dinners together or just sitting down for chats. He knew me and I knew him."

AAU and Asia Life expanded their geographical coverage in the 1920s, opening an office in Beijing and establishing agencies across China and in many other Asian cities. A new company, American International Underwriters (AIU), was established in New York in 1926, providing a balance to Starr's enterprises that was to prove invaluable when the Japanese invasion of China and other Asian countries cut short business in the Far East, at least for a few years.

When the war ended, AIU was the first foreign company to resume business in Shanghai, and the operation prospered until the changing situation in China in 1949 led to a transfer of the regional headquarters to Hong Kong. During the period when China was effectively closed to international business, K.K. Tse, by now AIG's regional head, retained contact with the PRC authorities.

AIG's pre-Revolution reputation and its ongoing contact, post-1949, with China led to an invitation in 1975 from the People's Insurance Company of China—the PICC—to visit the country. Hank Greenberg made the trip, accompanied by Mansfield Freeman's son, Buck Freeman (educated in Shanghai and founder of AIU's business in Japan), and Jimmy Manton (AIU's President, who led the company into many emerging markets). Even before the official Opening Up in 1978, AIG signed at the time of that 1975 visit a formal claims and reinsurance agreement with the PICC.

In July 1980, a representative office was opened in Beijing and this led, later that year, to the establishment of China America Insurance Company, a joint venture with the PICC, which was licensed to do business in the United States and Hong Kong, as well as in Beijing. In 1992, American International Assurance Company (AIA) was granted the first foreign insurance license in 40 years by the PRC, to operate a life insurance business in Shanghai, writing indigenous local business. This was complemented by a license to AIU to sell property and casualty policies to joint ventures and foreign enterprises, also in Shanghai. Then, in 1997, two further licenses were granted, which enabled AIA and AIU to operate from Guangzhou, selling policies like those in Shanghai. In May 1998, following extensive renovation, the AIA Building at Number 17, The Bund, was reopened and has since served as headquarters for the group's rapidly expanding China operations. In early 1999, the Chinese authorities informed AIG that the group would be permitted to expand its existing operations to two additional cities, Shenzhen and Foshan.

At the time of writing, the PRC government had granted licenses to 13 foreign insurance companies. That AIG was the first foreign insurer to receive permission to sell insurance policies in China (and will shortly have no fewer than six separate licenses) is a mark of AIG's success in China. "What accounts for this?" I ask Greenberg.

"I worked on it for 17 years," he replies. "You know, you can't rush China. I'll explain this in a moment. AAU and Asia Life had a great reputation before the war. We recruited and trained local people who became the managers of our business. We have shown long-term commitment to China. And we demonstrated this in tangible form, starting with the agreement with the PICC in 1975. During the 1980s, we built the Portman Centre in Shanghai. That was a visible presence in China—and our first office building was called the American International Building. Then I chaired the first international business advisory council for Zhu Rongji when he was Mayor of Shanghai. I spent considerable time on that for him, and I think we were quite helpful and valuable to the city of Shanghai and all the mayors who succeeded Zhu Rongji."

Greenberg is known for seeing to it that things get done immediately. His behavior is epitomized by Winston Churchill's wartime demand, "Action this day"—or even "Why wasn't it done yesterday?" Why, then, was he prepared to be so patient with China and take a long-term view?

"You have to look at the facts. China is a big country. It covers a huge part of the globe. It has 1.3 billion people. China is making dramatic progress, with change in almost every facet of human life. If you just go back to 1975, when I first went to China, and look at the progress made since then, China today is like another planet. Not only is the physical infrastructure of China changing, but also the lifestyle of the people has probably never been better at any time in their 5000-year history. Having said that, China still has a long way to go. But the speed at which they are making progress in every facet of life is remarkable. Even for those who criticize China's human rights policies, if they go back and look at China in 1975 and then look again at China today, the progress, including the field of human rights, has been enormous. When you feed and clothe and shelter 1300 million people, that is human rights, compared to what it was before. What China cannot tolerate is chaos. Chaos would destroy China. To create political instability in a country with that mass of population, until there is further progress and maturity in a political and social sense, would be quite wrong. Change will come. But it will come in China's time, not on or of a timetable of external forces.

"When I go to China, I see a nation that has made, in a brief period, just tremendous progress. Having said all that, I must add that if you want to do business in China, you need to take the long-term view. You have to be patient. China is, after all, a 5000-year-old civilization. They do not measure time in the same way that we do in the West. We want instant progress, instant change, instant everything. If you expect that in China, don't do business there because you simply won't succeed.

"I made many—I can't say how many—trips to China from 1975 to 1992, when we won our first license. That was an exercise in taking the long-term view. Most CEOs, when they think about doing business in China, make one or two trips and then expect everyone else to carry on for them. In China, like other parts of Asia, personal relationships are terribly important. If it becomes apparent that the relationship is being built just to benefit the foreigner, you might as well stay home."

Soon after our interview, Greenberg must leave to keep an appointment with Zhu Rongji. The Chinese premier is visiting the United States, and the top of his agenda is China's accession to the WTO. The economic crisis in East Asia, which began in 1997, has slowed China's growth. The state-owned enterprises, particularly those established in the 1950s and 1960s, are now in need of reform, and this will result in job losses and a heavy social cost. Unless new jobs are created, the change will take longer and it will be more painful. Foreign investment has started to wane as multinational corporations have begun to despair over the bureaucratic nature of the regulatory environment and the length of time typically needed to achieve profitable operations. Accession to WTO will result in an increase in trade with China, renewed foreign interest and investment, and pressure on the regulatory environment to change. Greenberg is optimistic that accession will present more opportunities for insurers such as AIG.

"So why has China taken so long to open up the financial services industry?" I ask.

"It has been slow for many reasons," says Greenberg. "China did not have the experience, the institutions, the regulations, or the knowledge base to deal with external financial institutions. They had to take it step by step, and they have had their fits and starts. But they are eager to learn, and they have had countless delegations here and there trying to gain an understanding of how to deal with today's financial institutions and the speed of global capital movement. If China had had a convertible currency when the Asia crisis began, it would have been a disaster. They were pursued by many and urged to inaugurate a convertible currency, but all those voices were very still when Asia had its problems. The best thing to happen was that China did not then have a convertible currency. In due course that will come, when China has the means and regulations to sustain a convertible currency. The same is true of financial institutions. My guess is that if China and the United States agree on WTO accession, there will be continued progress in opening the market to financial services—but it will be on a phased basis, as well it should be. They have learned a great deal in the last few years and they continue to learn. Hopefully, we will learn more about China and how to do business there."

Greenberg understands China, based on 25 years of experience in dealing with this market as chairman and CEO of AIG. Few chairmen of multinational companies have the luxury of this length of time in office. This continuity has been invaluable to AIG because the Chinese respect long relationships, and it has given AIG the ability to monitor developments in the country from a stable vantage point. Too often, global companies change their China management or board directors dealing with China after a relatively short period of time, thus losing experience that is essential to doing business in this unique market environment. "After all this time, and as the first insurer to obtain a license to do business in China, what are the secrets of success?" I ask.

"Well, you know, many," Greenberg responds. "I don't want to lay out a road map for everybody else. But we have credibility because we have done many things, over many years, that have made us known to and respected by the Chinese government. An important feature is that we have trained many Chinese, just as Starr did. We do have some expatriates, but most of the business is managed by Chinese. That's a key success factor, wherever we do business. I come back to the main point. You can't rush China. You have to take it step by step. That's the secret of success."

American International Group in China

AIG operates in Shanghai and Guangzhou, writing life insurance mainly for PRC nationals, and property and casualty (non-life) insurance for Sino-foreign joint ventures and wholly foreign-owned enterprises. It also provides reinsurance services where these businesses are concerned. Starting in 1999, AIG's operations extended to Shenzhen and Foshan.

The group employs over 800 people in Shanghai and Guangzhou and has almost 8000 agents working for AIA and AIU in these two cities.

3

A Shortage of Management

If they're too bureaucratic, you can't get anything done. If they're too entrepreneurial, you can't sleep at night.
JACK PERKOWSKI
CHAIRMAN & CHIEF EXECUTIVE
OFFICER, ASIMCO

ASIMCO is an unusual company. It was established specifically to acquire and operate businesses in China. Formed initially as an investment vehicle, it was the brainchild of a New York banker, Jack Perkowski, who had spent his life masterminding corporate transactions. After five years of intense activity and experience in the Chinese business environment, ASIMCO now has over US$400 million invested in China. The operations comprise 15 automotive components joint ventures, two wholly owned components companies, and two joint ventures in the brewing industry, including one of China's brand leaders, Five Star Beer.

Jack Perkowski lives in Beijing, although he enjoys returning to his farm in New Jersey. He has no doubt that the last five years in China have been the most challenging of his career, and no doubt that, if you are persistent, doing business in China can be both rewarding and fun because progress is very visible. His biggest chal-

41

lenge, he stresses, is caused by the huge shortage of indigenous executives in China, who are needed to manage businesses to an international standard. Addressing this shortfall is his key concern.

■ ■ ■

With his background as an independent adviser and deal maker, Jack Perkowski is able to analyze events in a clinical and objective manner. In the early 1990s, he remembers, the international press was euphoric about China and the amazing investment opportunities that were waiting for foreign companies to seize them. The ingredients were there for a bonanza—1.2 billion people, a government that was Opening Up the economy to outsiders, little local competition for the world's multinational corporations, a low cost-base economy in the middle of Asia that promised to be the up-and-coming region of the twenty-first century. What could go wrong?

In about 1996, he recalls, stories began to appear in the press about foreign businesses experiencing problems in China: regulatory uncertainty, difficulties with joint venture partners, copyright infringements, horrendously poor distribution channels, the emergence of fierce local competition. It was not his view that these problems were absent in 1993, 1994, and 1995—and then suddenly emerged in 1996 and 1997. "It was more the case that if a company had a problem in the early days, when the press was bullish about China, management was unlikely to talk about it, since this would point to something wrong with your company or your strategy, or the way you were doing business."

In fact, more companies had not only experienced much the same problems, but they had also begun to discuss them more openly with each other. This candor eventually spread to the press, where the problems were reported and a more realistic (and sometimes negative) mood developed toward China.

Perkowski sought to analyze the origin of the problems that he and others had encountered. "To me, it all boiled down to one issue: the lack of capable management to deal with the challenges." To explain this, he compares the managerial environment in the United States with that in China. "I start by looking at the universe of executives in the United States. After World War II—I pick that as a convenient timeframe—companies in the United States had to learn to be competitive as they sought to become global players, competing with their European and Japanese counterparts. In many cases, domestic and foreign competitors had inherent competitive advantages, so the U.S. companies had to become better at managing their businesses and therefore began to focus on improving management skills. 'Management' became a science in the developed countries of the world. Business schools were established and universities began offering MBA programs. Management development courses were prepared and conducted in many companies. These were designed to take raw managerial talent and provide enough structure to run a big company, while at the same time enabling managers to retain the entrepreneurial instincts necessary to drive the business forward."

Perkowski's hypothesis is that after 50 years of training and of treating management as a science in the United States and Europe, there is a large pool of managers capable of leading and managing major global companies. "If you were to plot the management universe in the United States, what you would get is a bell-shaped curve, where the vertical axis is the 'number of people' and the horizontal axis shows managerial behavior, which is categorized as 'bureaucratic' at one end and 'entrepreneurial' at the other. If you have a problem with management in the United States, you call up the headhunters, tell them what you want, and within a relatively short period of time you can have a team of people who are able to accomplish your objectives."

In China, Perkowski argues, exactly the opposite is true. From 1949 to 1978, during the period in which management was treated as a science in the West, China was a centralized economy closed to foreigners. As a result, no new domestic competition was created and foreign competition was kept out. In this context, the managers of Chinese enterprises were allocated capital and labor and told to make a certain product. They never had to learn how to optimize capital and labor. Once the product was manufactured, it was turned over to a state-run distribution company. So the manager of that enterprise never had to be responsive to the marketplace.

"As a result," Perkowski continues, "prior to 1978, virtually all managers in China would have been at the far left of the scale, very bureaucratic. On the other hand, in 1978, when Deng Xiaoping opened up the economy, the handcuffs were taken off. We all know that the Chinese are the most entrepreneurial people in the world. Beginning in 1978, a new class of managers was created, this time at the far right of the scale, very entrepreneurial. You saw it initially in the southern part of China, in Guangdong Province, next to Hong Kong. Now you see it all over China. Look at any city in China and you have evidence of an entrepreneurial spirit driving China forward."

"The problem for a company like ASIMCO, or for that matter any other multinational company, is that you cannot afford to be at either end of the management spectrum. If the management you have in China is too bureaucratic, you can't get anything done. On the other hand, if it is at the other end of the spectrum, you can't sleep at night because these cowboy entrepreneurs practice a brand of management that no multinational company would feel comfortable with. You might be in the components business today and find that you are in the hotel business tomorrow."

In China, therefore, there is at present a dearth of competent executives for companies such as ASIMCO. Perkowski argues that this is a temporary phenomenon and that within the next 10 to 15 years the PRC will develop its own cadre of managers capable of managing businesses to an international standard. Qinghua University in Beijing has started MBA courses; other business schools have opened their doors in the last three years; and many Chinese have taken management courses and are now gaining experience with multinationals. The problem is how to get through the next 10 years.

■ ■ ■

Perkowski has created a four-point action plan, which ASIMCO is implementing. First, try to identify the best available PRC managers from existing PRC enterprises. ASIMCO's strategy in China has been to grow its businesses in two sectors: automotive components and beer. The company chose the number 1 or number 2 enterprises in these sectors, theorizing that these enterprises had proved able to reach this ranking in their own domestically oriented industry and, therefore, might be capable of becoming successful in the global arena. ASIMCO began this strategy with the expectation that perhaps 50 percent of the PRC managers would prove capable of making the leap to the next level. In reality the success rate has been only on the order of 20 percent. "It's not so much the training, but the whole way of thinking that creates a hurdle for so many people."

The second strategy has been to supplement local management with experienced executives from Western countries. For ASIMCO, this was not so easy. Unlike most other foreign corporations doing business in China, there was no ready pool of talent waiting to be tapped. Executives had to be hired off the market, and this was obviously a higher-risk approach. A further problem that applies to all multinational corporations is the high cost of senior expatriates. When housing, hardship premium, schooling, medical care, and home leave visits are taken into account, the average annual cost of an expatriate package can be anything between US$300,000 and US$500,000—three to five times as much as in the home country. But it is not so much the absolute cost that causes the problem as the relative cost compared to the personnel cost of PRC nationals. In a factory that employs 1000 people, where the average annual wage cost per person is US$1,000, one expatriate can represent between 30 and 50 percent of total payroll cost. It is sometimes difficult for Chinese joint venture partners to swallow this. Even if they do, the individual must have superhuman qualities to convince them that he is worth this amount.

Perkowski points to a further inherent difficulty for the expatriate executive: "If you take a good company in China and try to make it into a good global company, it has to change—it can't stay the same. And, like most people, the Chinese don't welcome change. The argument that the Chinese use, at the level of general manager or deputy general manager, runs along these lines: 'Yes, those techniques and practices may work in Europe and the United States. But this is China. China is different.' They may actually believe that. Years of unfortunate contact with the foreigner have taught the Chinese that they are special. We agree that the Chinese are special. Everyone is special. But, we don't subscribe to the notion that because it works elsewhere it won't work in China. We think that, when you boil everything down, China actually operates in the same way as other places. The laws of economics apply here as they do in every part of the world. However, the fact that Chinese managers are able to argue in this way gives them an immediate excuse for not changing.

"In view of all this, we find that an expatriate must be quite outstanding. He has to have enough experience to overcome the credibility issue. He has to have had a substantial career prior to China—it's more difficult for someone just out of college or lacking experience. Second, he has to be an extremely patient person, yet very persistent—someone who does not take no for an answer. He has to be willing to roll up his sleeves. You have to find someone at a high level in an organization, with the relevant experience, who is the right kind of person and willing to come to China and do things he or she probably hasn't done for 10 or 15 years. We have great difficulty in finding those individuals. But they do exist and we have some great managers in ASIMCO. However, at the end of the day, our experience shows that we only have a 20 percent hit rate with the expatriates we bring to China. Perhaps other multinationals would score higher because they have refined their pool of talent over many years."

In 1998, the GE Pension Fund became a one-third shareholder in ASIMCO when Dean Witter, one of the original shareholders, was bought out. Part of the rationale for this was to give ASIMCO access to General Electric's proven managerial know-how and to compensate, with a long and proven record of managing in a global economy, for ASIMCO's lack of an organization outside China.

The third strategy is to hire from a growing pool of qualified PRC nationals. These are people who have experience, sometimes significant, of living and working in a foreign country for a multinational company, or who have worked for a multinational in China and have learned the international norms of corporate management and behavior. Many have trained overseas in MBA programs. In Perkowski's opinion, this group "understands the direction that China wishes to take, is less likely to resist change in an enterprise, and, of course, costs less. They have the advantage of being Chinese and of being trained in international management techniques. And they have none of the disadvantages of expatriates."

The fourth strategy is to train existing staff members. ASIMCO has done this, together with Caterpillar, with whom it has a cooperation agreement and a factory located in Shaanxi Province. Recruits for ASIMCO can come directly from Chinese universities, where the standard of education and training in engineering is excellent, in Perkowski's view. They can also come from other multinational companies, where they have been exposed to international work practices over the last five or so years, or from the management ranks of ASIMCO's joint ventures. ASIMCO now has a training center in Beijing, where staff members come for courses.

ASIMCO pursues all four routes to change managerial behavior and optimize the possibility of success. For Perkowski, age is currently a problem. "Someone over 40 has probably spent from 5 to 10 years during the Cultural Revolution in the fields, without formal education. This generation has grown up with the 'iron rice bowl' mentality. If Chinese managers come from a state enterprise, there is tremendous loyalty to the old ways of doing things, to the former organization, to the work unit. There is a need to divorce ownership from managerial control. This can be quite complicated to achieve. But I have great optimism, based on seeing the young talent joining our organization. They are the ones with the bright futures. For this group of people, our challenge is retention. As long as they see that they have opportunities for upward mobility, they won't change jobs for more compensation. By training and keeping these youngsters, this is how we eventually make up for China's present management shortage."

ASIMCO in China

Having invested US$400 million in China, ASIMCO has 17 joint ventures and two wholly owned companies there. Operating in two industry segments, automotive components and beer, the group had sales in 1998 of US$250 million.

4

Getting the Balance Right

We have shown respect to our Chinese partners. But, it is also important not to try to change yourself. You cannot be a Chinese. You were not born a Chinese and you cannot behave as a Chinese.
DR. MICHAEL PORTOFF
CHAIRMAN, BAYER (CHINA) LIMITED

Michael Portoff considers himself fortunate. In the early 1990s, he worked on Bayer's strategy for China at the company's German headquarters. In 1993 he was asked to implement that strategy, and he began by negotiating a cooperation agreement with the Ministry of Chemical Industries, which was signed in the Great Hall of the People in November 1993. Moving to Beijing in 1994, he was involved in the formation of no fewer than 12 joint ventures and the establishment of one of the first PRC holding companies.

For the last three years, he has lived in Hong Kong, directing both the operations on the mainland and Bayer's large China trading enterprise, based in the Special Administrative Region (SAR). With a turnover of almost $600 million, the combined operations of Bayer group companies in China and Hong Kong SAR employ over 2000 people. Dr. Portoff, who is German and who has a

French wife, has worked with Asia for 18 years, including a spell in Japan from 1985 to 1988. With this background and with these influences in his family and working life, he understands the need to respect local cultures and traditions without losing one's own identity. In his view, success in China is all about getting the balance right.

■ ■ ■

Bayer's involvement in China dates back to the 1880s, when the company exported to Asia its first products, primarily dye stuffs, from Germany. The first Bayer office in China was established in 1913, in Shanghai, and the first production facility was established in 1935, also in Shanghai, to produce pharmaceuticals, particularly Aspirin®. At that time, there were branches in Tianjin and Hankou, which is now part of Wuhan.

As a result of the Second World War and the Revolution in China in 1949, these activities ceased until after the Opening Up, when Bayer's first joint venture was established, in 1986, in Shanghai. Although this enterprise has since been sold as part of a larger corporate disposal, Bayer learned a great deal about China from this experience and from the smaller representative offices that the company established in other cities. In 1989, in the wake of the Tiananmen incident, the company's activities ceased temporarily, as was the case with other foreign businesses. However, in the early 1990s, as the second wave of investment into China started, Bayer's board of management and its business groups expressed increasing interest in the country and a major review of Bayer's China strategy was undertaken.

Business groups were encouraged to identify products that were sold or could be sold in China and in other Asian markets. As part of the strategy, a key principle was agreed early on, namely the need to protect these local sales in the longer term by planning for local production in China. Still further, Bayer recognized the need to be close to its customers and to participate in the economic life of the country—something only possible when there are domestic production capabilities. The thinking was clear and concise.

After agreeing upon a China strategy for the various business groups, a delegation from Bayer visited China in early 1993 and presented the strategy to the Ministry of Chemical Industries. The open and frank manner with which Bayer went about this was, in Dr. Portoff's view, part of the reason for the company's success thus far. He explains: "The Chinese have a certain mistrust of foreigners. After a history of 150 years through which China suffered at the hand of the foreigner, there are quite naturally some reservations. When we come to a new country, we have our own reservations about the people we meet. Should we trust each other? They don't look like us, and they certainly don't behave like us. Trust has to be built over a period of time. You can only achieve this if you do it in an open, honest, and frank way."

During 1993 and 1994, Bayer began negotiating the 12 joint ventures it now operates in China. This was done step by step, and the company's China executives learned many lessons that were used, through cross-fertilization, in subsequent negotiations. Dr. Portoff comments, "We cut short discussions with potential partners where the financial feasibility studies showed no realism or there was no meeting of the minds. However, in total, only four negotiations were terminated. We had to find the balance between the interests of Bayer and the relative strengths (and weaknesses) of our potential partners. Up to now, we have only signed up green field sites and haven't accepted to move into old premises that needed revamping. In addition, we have wanted large majority interests. We balanced the interest of the Chinese partner with the interest of Bayer, always in an open and frank manner. Potential problems were discussed at the outset, during the joint venture negotiations, rather than left to cause trouble after the joint venture was founded."

Bayer was one of the first foreign companies to establish a holding company in China, in September 1994. This indicated the level of commitment by Bayer to the PRC market. However, like other foreign companies, Bayer has encountered constraints in the use of its holding company. In China, holding companies cannot be used in the same way as in other countries—for example, for treasury activities, to optimize tax planning, or to act as a central service support to other operations in the country. However, Bayer has found that the holding company has proved to be an excellent strategic instrument and a general service company for the underlying joint ventures.

Bayer ensured that government authorities were kept informed of company developments at both a central and a local level. As Dr. Portoff puts it, "You have to establish good relations with the central authorities. In our case this was the Ministry of Chemical Industry, SINOPEC, MOFTEC, the State Planning Commission, and the Ministry of Health. However, if you deal only with the central government, you will not succeed, because the provinces have their own powers, proceedings, and wishes. It has been Bayer's policy to balance the two and to approach and inform both levels of government."

A homily that Dr. Portoff often preaches is the need to treat China with respect. "If you come to China with an arrogant manner, you are lost. You can learn a lot from the Chinese side. You may bring over technology or capital or branded products. However, you are in an unfamiliar environment; you have not grown up in China; you do not speak the language. How can you possibly understand the market and its needs? You have to learn the Chinese ways of doing things. They include:

- *Flexibility.* To survive, Chinese have learned to be flexible. Governments change. Laws and regulations change. Officials change. In the past, there was little stability in Chinese life.
- *Patience.* We cannot move as fast as we want or as fast as our head offices sometimes wish. In China, you must be patient. Things do not happen overnight. When it comes to choosing a joint venture partner, we have wanted to identify one for the longer term. As in a marriage, we wanted to choose the right partner and minimize the likelihood of eventual divorce. This takes time, and it is not just the courtship that can be lengthy. The average time taken by Bayer to establish a joint venture from the day the letter of intent is signed to

the day the business license is issued has been approximately
18 months.

- *Guanxi ('Relationship').* This is a famous word in China.
  Relationships are also important in the West, but they are
  still more important in China and one of the principles of
  success in all walks of life. The problem is that individuals
  come and go, and therefore you have to develop something
  I call 'institutional *guanxi*.'
- *Respect.* Regardless of our ownership percentage, we have
  tried to treat our joint venture partners as equals. We have
  discussed problems face to face, sometimes for many hours.
  We have never put anything to the vote.
- *Ethics.* I can honestly say that in all of our projects, we have
  never come across one instance where international ethics
  have been questioned. Corruption is not a word that, mer-
  cifully, I have ever had to use to describe behavior we
  encountered."

Bayer now has manufacturing capabilities in many cities in
China, including Beijing, Chengdu, Nanjing, Qingdao, Shanghai,
and Wuxi. Most were established with midsized investments of up
to US$30 million each. They are engaged in activities in the chem-
ical, medical, and image technology industries. Currently, the focus
is on consolidation, on trying to develop these operations past the
start-up phase to achieve profitability. However, in light of its experience in the last 12 years, Bayer is now ready for a further period
of investment and is considering larger projects—for example a
polycarbonate plant in Shanghai that would require a total investment of up to US$500 million. Other projects in the polymer sec-
tor will also be considered.

On a more philosophical note, Dr. Portoff believes in the
importance of understanding the culture and history that have
brought China to where it is today. The different approaches of
Buddhism, Confucianism, Taoism, and Maoism have all con-
tributed to the complex values and patterns of behavior of con-
temporary China. To be successful, the multinational executive

must understand these to a certain extent. A reading of Chinese history is de rigueur. The Chinese are proud of their history. You in turn have to respect it. This does not mean that Chinese ways are the only methods that a multinational company must adopt in China. Quite the contrary, according to Dr. Portoff. "You don't have to change yourself. We come as Europeans. I am proud of my own history and background. In the West we draw from Christian, Jewish, Greek, and Roman cultural achievements and values, while China's roots and historical experience offer a quite different heritage. My approach is never to compare—better, worse—but to recognize differences and leave it at that. See the differences, but do not to try to change yourself. You cannot be a Chinese. You were not born a Chinese; you cannot behave as a Chinese; and you should not imitate."

For this reason, Bayer China has put localization high on its list of objectives. PRC staff are recruited for managerial positions not only because of their technical capabilities or business experience, but because of their grasp of Chinese culture and the operating environment. They are then trained on the job and sent to neighboring Asian countries or overseas for further training and work experience. On their return, the expectation is that they will replace expatriates, who complete their tours of duty after an average of three or four years. Ultimately, Bayer wants most of its executives in China to be PRC nationals, to take advantage of their knowledge of the local market and business environment. Dr. Portoff wants the responsible positions to be filled by Chinese managers.

Bayer China has focused on trying to build a professional environment and to reward progress not through higher pay but through greater responsibility. This strategy has resulted in a very low turnover of personnel. In fact, there has been practically no staff turnover in the holding company since it was founded in 1994. Dr. Portoff considers that his staff are aware of the benefits of the training provided by Bayer and of the career structure that offers them opportunities to progress within Bayer's organization in China.

As for many multinationals operating in China, while the long-term vision is clear, the pressures for short-term financial performance are ever-present. For Dr. Portoff, this is a matter of clear communication with the head office. "A short-term approach is unrealistic in this country. There may be a few short-term successes—for example, companies in the consumer products industry. However, for companies like ours, with a capital-intensive profile, you have to be patient, to wait a little and focus on mid- and long-term goals. The worst thing you can do in China is to rush.

"Short-term losses can lead to a negative impression. And the press is sometimes negative about China—for example, over human rights, Tibet, and Taiwan. But these negative views do not reflect the changes that have occurred in China over the last 20 years and the true potential of the country. It is wrong to be either euphoric or negative. Neither viewpoint is correct. The picture is very complex in this country. Therefore, you have to paint a realistic picture to your board of management. You must not conceal or withhold the difficulties, the problems, and the challenges. This is not a champagne-drinking country. It is still a place for the pioneer. You have to roll your sleeves up. In our presentations at Bayer's head office, we have referred to China as a 'giant with certain weaknesses.' It is not an Eldorado, and it is not a country without hope. If this is how you describe it, then people will not have unrealistic expectations. In addition, you absolutely need the backing of your board of management at home and of the executives at headquarters. Otherwise, you cannot work in these difficult and complex surroundings."

An illustration in an international magazine recently portrayed a ship about to be swept into a whirlpool, with an accompanying caption saying something on the order of "Is China next?" To Dr. Portoff, this displayed a lack of understanding of China and its present position along a continuum of change. "The structural issues that exist in China today existed many years ago. They are being tackled piecemeal by a very determined and smart group of leaders. I am optimistic about China. I have seen the changes over the last seven years. They started with simple things, such as the availability of consumer goods in cities like Beijing and Shanghai. But these are now not confined to the top two or three cities—you see modern products now in places like Chengdu, Chongqing, Harbin, and Wuhan. Unlike 10 years ago, Beijing and Shanghai, at least, are no longer extreme-hardship postings for expatriates.

"I have also seen in the few years a change in the minds of the authorities at the central, provincial, and municipal levels. They have opened up. It started from the outside—in their choice of clothing, in how they appeared. But they have also changed from the inside—they have more openness, much more understanding of economic patterns and behavior. The country today cannot be compared with the old Communist states such as the former Soviet Union or East Germany. It is totally different. If you go to Beijing or Shanghai, you will not meet Mr. Marx or Mr. Engels or Mr. Hegel on the streets. This is a capitalistic country, more like what you would have seen in Manchester at the end of the nineteenth century. I am no longer surprised when a first-time visitor, a friend who stays with us for 10 days or so, reports to me after the first few days, 'Oh, this isn't what I expected.' He immediately becomes an ambassador for China back home. Everybody is surprised at the normal daily life. And this makes me very optimistic.

"China remains, however, a complex country in which to do business. It has a different history and a different approach to doing business. These differences will not wash away. They will remain. When you form and operate a joint venture, the emphasis has to be on the word 'joint.' You have to understand that there are different points of view. But this doesn't mean that you have to give in. To succeed, you have to get the balance right."

Bayer in China

Bayer conducts its China import and warehousing activities in Hong Kong through Bayer China Co. Ltd. Four liaison offices on the mainland—in Beijing, Shanghai, Guangzhou, and Chengdu—provide technical support. In addition, there are other Bayer companies in Hong Kong with similar activities; these are Dystar China Ltd., Agfa Hong Kong Ltd., and Bayer Diagnostics Ltd.

In mainland China, the Bayer Group has 12 joint ventures, one wholly foreign-owned company, and a holding company. The activities are located in Beijing, Shanghai, Wuxi, Nanjing, Qingdao, and Chengdu. Investment to date totals over US$220 million.

Bayer has more than 2100 employees in the PRC and Hong Kong SAR. Total sales in 1998 reached US$600 million from sales of products in the following business areas: pharmaceuticals, diagnostic systems, crop protection agents, plastics, synthetic rubber, rubber chemicals, fibers, dyes, pigments, organic and inorganic intermediates, photographic films, and electronic imaging systems.

5

Building the Team

*Waking them up at 3:00 A.M. for
a conference meeting was a totally
unreasonable request. But for those that
got up, we wrote their names down.*
JERRY NORSKOG
CHAIRMAN, JOHNSON & JOHNSON
CHINA INVESTMENT LIMITED

Xi'an, the capital of Shaanxi Province, is well known as the ancient capital of China, comparable in stature with Rome and Constantinople. Since 1974, when an army of terra-cotta warriors was uncovered at a 2000-year-old imperial burial complex about 20 miles outside Xi'an, the locale has also become one of China's main tourist attractions.

In a modern suburb of this dusty city is an area dedicated to medical research and the manufacture and sale of traditional Chinese medicines. This is the location of one of China's most successful Sino-foreign joint ventures, Xian-Janssen.

The success of Xian-Janssen is due both to Johnson & Johnson's foresight and timing and to the energy and imagination of Jerry Norskog and his management team. Norskog hails from the United States but is of Norwegian origin. This explains his Scandinavian surname and also his Viking stature. Of the 25 years he has worked for Johnson & Johnson, 16 have been in Asia, including seven in China. After working for two years in Xi'an on the formation of Xian-Janssen, Norskog then spent five years in Beijing developing for Johnson & Johnson one of the best sales and marketing teams in the People's Republic of China.

In Norskog's view, what separates winners from losers in China is the foreign company's approach to developing people. Johnson & Johnson has a worldwide reputation for the success of its corporate culture. In this chapter, we record the key features of Johnson & Johnson's approach to developing its people in China.

■ ■ ■

"When I interview a new recruit, I ask him what advice his father and mother gave him about being successful in life. The answer is usually: 'Keep your head down, keep your mouth shut, ensure you have a good relationship with your boss, be obedient, and work hard.' Now I am going to ask him to stand up, to speak out heretical ideas, to fight intellectually, to challenge his boss. I am going to tell him that risk taking is rewarded, not punished. I am literally going to turn the tables on him. He is going to have to make a 180-degree turn if he is to meet my expectations."

The problems facing multinational corporations, in terms of the deficiency of human resources, are graphically illustrated by Jerry Norskog. For all international businesses trying to succeed in China, the key constraint is people.

China's universities are of a high academic standard. They have produced engineers capable of building the world's largest hydroelectric plant in the Yangtze River, rocket scientists who can put satellites into space, and economists who can produce 8 percent growth in GPD consistently for 20 years. But there are deficiencies in the raw material that academic education cannot easily remove. Norskog explains, "The talented youngsters who are the fine products of these fine universities are also the sons and daughters of the Communist past. They have grown up in work units. Their reference point is the 'iron rice bowl.' They learn by rote, they write it all down and memorize it, and then regurgitate what they have learned when asked a question. They are very good at memorizing data and at assimilating facts and ideas, but they have not been trained to be free thinkers."

The social and cultural background is not one that well serves the needs of a large international company. Most recruits were single children. The parents were typically separated for years during the Cultural Revolution, although they are now living together again. As a child, your new hire may well have had four doting grandparents all to himself. His values are Confucian. The Chinese have a wonderful saying which translates into English as "fat pigs get eaten," which basically means that if you draw attention to yourself, you'll be singled out and penalized. In Norskog's words, "This is precisely what I am asking a new recruit to be: I am asking him to be a fat pig. This is like asking someone to jump off a building and telling him that it's going to be okay."

For Johnson & Johnson, the task was how to create a sales and marketing network across China with district managers in 50 cities in five years. In the United States or in Europe, this would have been a tough assignment, but with the backgrounds of the bright graduates from China's universities, the job was even harder. In Norskog's view, the time allocated in China to accomplish this type of task should be longer, perhaps seven or eight years, because of the cultural, educational, social, and economic backgrounds of the manager candidate material. However, Johnson & Johnson did not have the luxury of time. In China, as in the rest of the world, speed is the key to competitive advantage.

A profile was developed of the perfect candidate and a program was devised to identify the right recruits, train them fast, and select future leaders. The techniques used were well tested in the West, but in China they needed "Chinese characteristics." First, recruitment. Johnson & Johnson searched for the best minds in the country. They visited the best universities and colleges. They put to work the concept of a "career day," sometimes with interesting results.

As Norskog recalls, "In 1992, in Xi'an, we decided to hold a career day. We sold the idea to our local PRC management at the factory, who had never heard of a career day. We told them that we would go to the best universities in Xi'an and ask for the top three graduating class members in key departments, and we would invite this group to come to our company for a full day. We planned to provide a number of lectures to this group about the industry and our company, with a focus on career opportunities. We were going to offer exhibits, featuring each of our internal departments, on tables in our cafeteria. Manning these exhibits would be the managers of each of our key departments. They would develop detailed materials on their individual departments and would answer questions. That was the concept. Of course, nobody had ever heard of it; it had never been done before. But we managed to get everything sorted out and went to see all the deans of the schools and the heads of the major academic departments.

"The night before the career day was scheduled to be held—it must have been 10 or 11 P.M.—I received a call from the Chairman of the Board, who told me that the Party Secretary was terribly upset about what we had planned; that our posters had been taken down at all the universities; and that substitute notices had been put up, saying that anyone attending the career day would be in trouble. I got up, dressed, and with some key colleagues went into discussions, which ultimately led us to the Vice Governor.

"During the long discussions, which lasted well into the night, we finally convinced all the concerned parties. Some time before the sun came up, we concluded that to build the 'Socialist Market with Chinese characteristics,' according to Deng Xiaoping, it perhaps no longer made sense to send the brightest and best graduates from universities to the countryside for an education. Perhaps, instead, it made sense to send them to enterprises that had modern management and new technology so that they could be trained and become leaders in the socialist market economy. As a consequence, we delayed the program by a week. The participation from the Party, from government officials, and also from professors and deans of the universities increased. We had almost 75 more people than we originally planned, due to the renewed interest and to the recognition that a new model was being tried out."

Recruitment came first. Second, Johnson & Johnson focused on training and on manager selection and development. While over 100 new graduates were recruited each year, these were divided into groups of 50 who trained together. The concept of "management camp" was developed. It was a small-scale "Outward Bound," somewhat military in design and reminiscent of programs used by the U.S. Marines and other military institutions the world over. Working as part of the team was Chong Siong Hin, a former drill sergeant in the Singapore Special Forces. The Chinese take well to such concepts, since much of the country's schooling reflects the military (e.g., morning parades, cadres of young pioneers being disciplined as part of their induction into the Party, etc.).

Norskog continues: "Chong and I created an environment that was very competitive, very aggressive, just a bit over the top, just a bit crazy—an environment that expected just a bit more than it was reasonable to expect. These camps would provide us with an opportunity to really observe behavior and traits of character which, in a one-on-one interview or in a resume, don't jump out at you. In these annual camps, we identified our potential leaders. They are held in the mountains. At a typical camp, everybody is in formation at 6:00 A.M. I lead—the President leads—the warm-up exercises. We jog three kilometers, come back and have 15 minutes to change clothes, half an hour to eat breakfast, and then we are in the classroom. We have a few short breaks during the day. We developed a very interactive, competitive training program, which rewarded the kinds of behavior we wanted to see. For example, we rewarded people who stood up and shouted out their views. We rewarded people for taking initiative and for taking risks. We stimulated the kinds of behavior that we value as a company, in stark contrast to 'face' and other Confucian values.

"Just imagine a week where you are exercising at 6:00 A.M. and seldom finish before 11 at night. In a 10-day camp, on perhaps three nights at least, we would go to two or three in the morning—as I said, a bit over the top, expecting more than is realistic—to determine who is ready for the types of challenges our company offers.

"And then change—constant, constant change. For example, we would say, 'Okay, break into teams. We want a 20-page letter to the Chairman of the Board on this subject and it's due the day after tomorrow.' The next morning we would say, 'The Chairman doesn't speak Chinese, the letter has to be in English, and 20 pages are too much—he says he will only read 10—and it is due tonight instead of tomorrow.' Then, at around lunchtime, we would say that the chairman has decided to visit camp; he is arriving by air this afternoon; but he can't stay long, so he only wants three slides in English. Change, change, change—it drives them nuts.

"Perhaps the most telling test came about halfway through the second week at three in the morning. We would arrange for someone to knock on the dormitory doors and shout that everybody had to come downstairs for a conference, in full business dress, as soon as possible because a special meeting had been called. At that point, you really start to see the cream separate from the milk. Most people found that request totally unreasonable and would give logical reasons why they could not come downstairs. But we recorded the names of those who did come down. They were the winners.

"For all of the recruits, this was an incredible, exhausting, exhilarating learning experience, a 'change your life' experience, and many of them loved it. Like the U.S. Marines, Chong and I challenged them early, and we also cut our losses early. Many said this is not for me—not my cup of tea. So, up front, we were able to identify people who were interested in our culture. This saved a great deal of time."

Norskog's approach to team selection and team building works well for a company like Johnson & Johnson that has clear and established values—values that are well-articulated, well-understood, and "lived." Johnson & Johnson's values statement is an essential part of the corporate philosophy. Thus, the messages given during camp training are in accord with the culture experienced later in the office.

This military approach works well for the Chinese, who understand the benefits in terms of efficiency of a strong command environment. It seems that the Johnson & Johnson experience builds on and molds, rather than altogether replaces, the existing value system of PRC nationals. New hires can therefore understand the application of partially familiar values within Johnson & Johnson. Residential training delivers clear messages and furthers the formation of strong bonds. As Johnson & Johnson found, it can be highly effective.

Over the past seven years, the company has created an enviable team, but, as is only to be expected, not one without problems. Retention has proved to be a key issue, caused in part by a lack of patience in many recruits and in part by competitors poaching the most successful young managers. The issue of patience deserves exploration. On the one hand, the Chinese have great pride in their abilities, as they should. On the other hand, they completely underestimate how much ground they lost during the years between 1949 and 1979, when contact with the West was limited. There is an expectations gap. The young, intelligent, hardworking people don't really understand what they missed and don't understand how complex managing a modern business really is. Consequently, they tend to underestimate how long it takes to reach so-called international standards and how much work is involved.

Johnson & Johnson built a reputation for effective training, and Xian-Janssen built a reputation as one of China's most successful Sino-foreign joint ventures. Companies that came later to China wanted to buy this experience, and Norskog found that some organizations used to book rooms at the hotel next to the Xian factory to interview his employees. He adds, "I would be surprised to hear of a single big pharmaceutical company in China that doesn't have at least one ex-Xian-Janssen executive on its management board— and we're very proud of that."

A feature that Norskog considers an important element in the company's success was trying to take the "foreignness" out of training. It was not "here's another foreign idea." "If we wanted to talk about leadership, we did not refer to Drucker or Harvard, we referred to Sun Tzu or the first Emperor of China. We looked back into Chinese history to find appropriate examples of leadership. We even used Mao Tse-tung's Red Book, in a totally apolitical way, to look at leadership and communication. We studied the Romans and Emperor Qin Shihuang in an effort to show how we were going to build a national network and develop a chain of command. We asked how our generals in Chengdu were going to be managed and rewarded. This was not only fun but, more important, it created a great deal of pride in our Chinese staff. We never tried to create an American company. We wanted to build a global company with Chinese characteristics."

Johnson & Johnson in China

Johnson & Johnson has seven operating entities in China, three joint ventures, two wholly owned enterprises, and two branches. Products manufactured and sold in China include pharmaceutical products, bandages (Band Aid), sutures (Ethicon), and analgesic cough–cold products.

6

Leading the Change through Partnership

In China, if you build the right
relationships with your partners—
ministers, government officials, your
joint ventures, your customers, and
your people—you can understand their
objectives better and help them by leading
the changes that are happening so fast in
our industry and in this great country.
DR. RANDOLPH TZU-YU YEH
CHAIRMAN, LUCENT TECHNOLOGIES
CHINA CO. LTD

Randy Yeh has an unusual background for someone leading the China operations of one of the world's largest multinational corporations—he was born in China.

That says as much about Lucent's foresight in choosing the head of its China business as it does about Dr. Yeh's abilities. It might seem strange that there are few Chinese-born chairmen of multinational corporation operations in China, but the cause is clear: a lack of international and business experience among executives raised in the PRC who, on the basis of age, would now be ready for leading roles. Randy Yeh was different. Although he was born in Qingdao, on China's eastern seaboard, he was educated in Taiwan, where he received a bachelor of science degree in physics, and then in the United States, where he earned a Ph.D. in computer science from the University of Texas at Austin. Thereafter, the first 17 years of his working life were spent outside the mainland of China.

Dr. Yeh joined AT&T Bell Laboratories in 1978 as a member of the technical staff working on the 5ESS switching system. After several promotions, in 1990 he was sent to Japan in a business development role that was followed in 1992 by his becoming Country President of AT&T Taiwan for three years. During this period, he turned the business into a profitable enterprise, and in 1994 he won for AT&T the Taiwan National Quality Award and the Best Foreign Business Award. It was a natural move, in 1995, for him to welcome a posting to China, the country of his roots, where he became the first Chinese-American to be appointed an officer of AT&T. After the restructuring of AT&T in 1996, he became the first Chairman of Lucent Technologies China.

Because of his experience of working in both Asian and American cultures, Dr. Yeh has good insight into the key success factors for a company such as Lucent in China. This has been amply demonstrated in his current role. When he took up his present position, Lucent's business in China was heavily in the red. By the end of 1998, all of Lucent's operations in China were profitable, and revenues are currently growing at more than twice the market rate as market share increases.

By international standards, Lucent was a late entrant to the China market. Only after Lucent's predecessor parent corporation,

AT&T, was broken up by the U.S. government in 1984 was AT&T permitted to conduct business outside the United States. Consequently, while many telecommunications supply companies established joint ventures in the PRC during the 1980s, it was not until 1993 that a Memorandum of Understanding was signed between AT&T and the former State Planning Commission. After the second restructuring of AT&T in 1996, Lucent Technologies was created, and, together with Bell Laboratories (its research and development brain), Lucent was able to take advantage of the global communications revolution. Greater focus was given to emerging markets such as China, particularly in the area of network planning, which is one of the corporation's core strengths.

■ ■ ■

Dr. Yeh is keen to point out the opportunity in his native land. In a talk given in Paris, he remarked, "France is a highly developed nation, respected for its telecom infrastructure, in which it has done a great job over the past century. By comparison, China has come recently to telecommunications and is currently putting in equipment that is the size of the network in France once every two years. It is a huge market. In 1998, there were 22 million new subscribers. That's roughly the size of the total subscriber base in either Canada or Australia and New Zealand combined. And it will remain a huge market for the next 20 or 30 years." To illustrate the importance that Lucent attaches to the China market, the corporation has divided the world outside North America into four geographical regions: Europe and Africa, South America, Asia-Pacific—and China.

Of course, it is not just the additional 22 million lines a year that are creating change in China. The state-owned carrier, China Telecom, is being delinked from its sponsoring government department, the newly formed Ministry of Information Industry. The PRC government is fostering competition and in the near future will break the China Telecom monopoly into several independent companies. New regulations are coming out, aimed at gradually creating a more open and competitive market environment. Cable may play a part in the future and so will Unicom, the nascent second national carrier, as well as, potentially, a third telecom company, China Great Wall, established to use the frequency owned by the People's Liberation Army.

Dr. Yeh forecasts, "The communications industry and information technology are going to touch, like it or not, everyone's life on this earth—and for the better. At Lucent, we are in the middle of this change, and blessed by Bell Laboratories' technology. China's 1.3 billion people are just starting to go through this tremendous change. Many are experiencing electronic communications for the first time, often with wireless coming first. The telecom market in China is growing fast, and the technology is changing fast. There is, in fact, continuous change. In Lucent, we like change—we embrace it, we anticipate it, and we try to lead it. Here in China, we are in the middle of a communications revolution. For me, for Lucent, it is the opportunity of a lifetime. We can make a win/win contribution to our shareholders and to the PRC."

Dr. Yeh is passionate about his chosen industry and the benefits he sees that it brings to mankind. However, he becomes equally passionate when speaking of the importance of developing good relationships with one's partners. In his view, in the unique environment of China you have to consider five levels: (1) central government leaders and ministers, (2) local government officials, (3) joint venture partners, (4) customers, and (5) employees.

He begins, "Lucent has its global headquarters in the United States, in Murray Hill, New Jersey, and of course we are registered in the United States. We are viewed in China as an American company. For any American company, whether low tech, medium tech, or high tech, a sound, stable, and good relationship between the U.S. and the PRC is key to business success in China. Since I took over as head of operations here, I have tried to show that Lucent is not just a strong global high technology company, but also a friend to China. At Lucent, we try to help foster a more constructive relationship between the United States, the great superpower, and the PRC, the great emerging superpower."

Lucent has tried to improve communications and understanding between the Chinese and the Americans, through, for instance, involvement in the Joint Conference on Commerce and Trade (JCCT) and through the U.S.–China Business Council. Dr. Yeh points out, "It doesn't hurt anyone to increase communication. In many cases, when we increase communication we have a better understanding of each other's position. While we may continue to have differences, and they may sometimes be substantial, we might still find them acceptable. We try to demonstrate that we take a long-term approach to China and that we have China's interests at heart, as well. In 1997, we established two Bell Laboratories in China, one in Beijing and the other in Shanghai. Bell Labs, which in our view has the finest communications technology in the world, has received eight Nobel prizes to date."

President Jiang Zemin has visited Bell Laboratories on two occasions. On the most recent visit, in 1997, he penned his own message in Chinese calligraphy: "To launch a new sphere of cooperation in high technology." The Chinese leader has always shown that he is willing to welcome senior Lucent executives during their visits to the PRC and to discuss technology and recent innovations.

By working with government ministries, Lucent is able to understand China's telecommunications objectives and to work in partnership to find solutions. Dr. Yeh applies this philosophy equally to Lucent's customers, China Telecom and Unicom, and to its joint venture partners. "By having a good relationship, we can be on the inside and we can anticipate change. We can understand the impact of new regulations quickly and we can see how new end-customer patterns are emerging—for example, Internet usage in China and the convergence of voice and data. We have a better chance of assessing when things are likely to happen in this marketplace."

Dr. Yeh cites two recent examples of successful partnerships with customers. "Following the signing of the Memorandum of Understanding with the former Ministry of Post and Telecommunications (MPT) in December 1995, we have worked closely with

China Telecom. China Telecom emphasizes technology leadership, and they are very good at building the networks. So we explored standards together. They visited Bell Labs. After that, we developed together a plan to build a DWDM (Dense Wavelength Division Multiplexing) transmission link between Wuhan and Xi'an. It has been a great success, generating 10 gigabits a second of transmission capability, which is the highest in China. After this experiment, China Telecom decided to adopt DWDM technology for its entire transport network. This is an example of a win/win partnership. It will enable China Telecom to embrace change and allow us to be part of these developments.

"Unicom is a new operator, formed four years ago as the second carrier. The company relies much more on others to provide technical consultancy and turnkey solutions, and they are open to the solution concept. So we have embarked on a new concept ourselves by offering joint market analysis and joint network planning. We worked together with Unicom's leaders and people and helped them work out, in this changing time, in this changing market, what they can do—what services they need to provide, and at what speed, in order to differentiate themselves so that they can be the choice of their customers. We have helped them plan their first long-distance network, which provides a solution that differs from the solution adopted by China Telecom. This new approach draws on Lucent's capacity to offer complete end-to-end solutions, including network planning, to our customers."

Like all other multinational corporations in China, Lucent finds that hard work is required to make joint ventures successful. "It's a challenge," says Dr. Yeh. "But I want to stress one thing: You have to look at it from the other person's point of view. You will always have differences, but if you act fairly, frankly, and honestly, you can make a joint venture succeed. When there is fairness on both sides, frank discussion can happen and a relationship can be built. Understanding can be established and trust will develop. Once you have trust, many things can work in China. When you try to negotiate a contract, for instance, in a very formal fashion, there could be many difficulties. But if you get to know each other well, you can become friends and trust each other. You can have a sound understanding and then many things can be put on the table, looked at from both parties' angles, and get resolved. The final solution may be different from what you initially conceived, but your partner in China is capable of thinking of very creative ways in China to meet your needs. You can develop a win/win partnership."

Giving weight to Dr. Yeh's arguments, all six of Lucent's joint ventures in China have been profitable since 1997. Four of them are among the joint ventures with the best return on investment in the telecommunications industry in China in 1997.

Another theme, echoed by many leaders of multinational corporations in China, is the importance of localization, not just to improve responsiveness and costs, but to allow Lucent to compete more effectively in a fiercely competitive industry. In Dr. Yeh's view, this is as much about developing local talent as about localizing processes and functions. "My feeling is that we still need to spend more energy and time to develop the overall skills of our people. There is still a significant experience gap between our Chinese employees and their counterparts, for instance, in the United States. We have established training and career development plans for all employees to demonstrate to our people that we are serious and that we have their long-term interest at heart. We have also repeatedly communicated our corporate values—for example integrity, focus on results, customer dedication, and care about the communities we work and live in—in order to build the right spirit and behavior in our people and in our business."

Concerning the right spirit, it is worth noting that Lucent has been an active supporter of Project Hope, a charity that helps underprivileged children go to school. The corporation has sponsored a project in a village some three hours from Beijing, in neighboring Hebei Province, where a new school has been built and many children have been "adopted" and supported by Lucent employees and their families. Dr. Yeh is proud to relate, "Every two or three months we go together to see these kids, their families, and the teachers. Sometimes we take the children out to Beijing to see educational exhibits, such as the aquarium. Sometimes we help by donating libraries and organizing computer training for the teachers, or by planting trees. Over the years, this has become quite an event in the village. Now, every time we go, the whole village turns out to see us. This has been a great experience for our employees and their families who have joined in this activity. By doing this together under the name of Lucent Technologies, they really feel proud of what we stand for."

Dr. Yeh concludes, "So we try to build partnerships with our employees, with our joint venture partners, with our customers, and then with the government and its ministers. If we can get this right, we can work with people in China to make change happen—and we can put ourselves in a position where Lucent is leading that change."

Lucent in China

Lucent Technologies currently has seven regional offices, six joint ventures, and two wholly owned companies in China, with over 3000 employees.

Headquartered in Murray Hill, New Jersey, Lucent Technologies designs, builds, and delivers a wide range of public and private networks, communications systems, data networking systems, business telephone systems, and microelectronic components. Bell Laboratories is the company's research and development arm.

7

Controlling the Uncertainties

*When Jiang Zemin wakes up in the
morning, his biggest concern is how he
feeds 1.2 billion people.*
TERRENCE BARNETT
COUNTRY HEAD, NOVARTIS CHINA

Novartis is one of the world's leading life sciences companies.
Formed in December 1996 by the merger of two Swiss-based
companies, Ciba-Geigy and Sandoz, Novartis holds top positions
internationally in pharmaceuticals, agrochemicals, and specialized
nutritional products. Headquartered in Basel, Switzerland, Novartis
has a small home market and to grow and prosper must focus on
markets in other countries. China, with its huge population, represents an opportunity that companies such as Novartis cannot afford
to ignore.

Terry Barnett is British by birth and worked extensively in
Africa, Europe, and the Middle East before being appointed in
1996 to head up Novartis operations in China. With the benefit of
having worked in many countries, he is well-placed to spot the
uncertainties and how these can be controlled, and also used to
advantage.

As a company engaged in health care and agriculture, Novartis is subject to the uncertainties of government policy and regulation, as well as those inherent in any commercial environment. In China, with the change from a centrally planned to a market economy, this adds a further dimension to the challenge of creating a profitable enterprise. Barnett outlines some of the uncertainties of operating in the PRC and the ways in which he seeks to control them.

■ ■ ■

In the pharmaceuticals industry you are always close to government. Like education and defense, health care is a major concern for all governments. Hence there is regulation—of patents, of the approval of drugs for safety and effectiveness, of prices charged to hospitals, and sometimes of the royalties and rates of return earned by pharmaceutical companies. The agricultural industry is also subject to government interest, and therefore regulation, if only because in many countries farming is an industry that commands political attention. In China, as in many other countries, both the pharmaceuticals industry and the agrochemicals industry receive special government attention because of the direct impact they have on the well-being of the people.

As Barnett explains, "The foreign pharmaceuticals companies have brought products to China that were previously unavailable. Western drugs have therapeutic effects not available from Chinese medicines. We came with drugs that can handle diseases in areas that were previously untreatable, except with certain Chinese medicines of limited efficacy. I am speaking about cancer, heart diseases, and other such ailments.

"As a result of this, and because of the structure of the health care industry in China, the foreign companies have taken a large share, within a short period of time, of the pharmaceuticals market in China in value terms. I mention the structure of the industry in China, because pharmaceuticals account for a significant proportion of total health care costs, primarily because of the limited investment in medical facilities, particularly in outpatient care and in the compensation of doctors. As a result, foreign pharmaceuticals companies receive more attention than would otherwise be the case."

Agrochemicals and seeds are perhaps just as sensitive. Barnett remembers an interview with President Jiang Zemin on CNN. When asked what concerned him most when he woke up in the morning, the head of state replied, "I worry about feeding one and a quarter billion people." Barnett expands on this concern: "With its horrendous famines in the 1930s and after the Revolution, during the Great Leap Forward, China's leaders are obsessed with the objective of self-sufficiency in food. China wants the security of having all of its agricultural products and inputs grown or made in China. This has led to the encouragement in agrochemicals of synthesis plants, to make the basic substance that is then formulated into the final product."

With government so prominent in the industries in which Novartis China operates, developing a good relationship with and staying close to government is a necessity. The President of Novartis is a regular visitor to China to meet the Chinese head of state and key ministers. Novartis wishes to be seen as a friend of China, working jointly on pharmaceutical and agricultural research projects. Trying to work with government, and thereby spotting the policy changes, is part of reducing the uncertainties inherent in this environment.

While China has opened its doors quite considerably over the last 20 years, in many areas trade is still restricted. As Barnett observes, "We all welcome China as a member of the World Trade Organization. But there is probably overconfidence about the impact of WTO on our ability to do business in China in a freer manner, because WTO membership doesn't automatically confer that freedom. It will take time. There will be phase-in periods in different markets, and these could be relatively long. You only have to look at what the Europeans did with Japanese cars to realize that phase-in periods even in a region like Europe can be long—cars were governed by a 15-year agreement."

"We all need to appreciate where China is coming from and that it is going through the most dramatic and massive economic transformation ever attempted in history, in any country. In a country of this size, which has been closed to the outside world for decades, as foreigners we should be sympathetic to Chinese concerns. They fear that we will enter the market and exploit the economy, using our business skills which at this point are greater than those of Chinese enterprises. It will take some time before the Chinese are confident that their companies are capable of going head-to-head against the large multinationals. I would very much like to see the first big Chinese multinationals succeed locally and then on the world stage. All of us would benefit because the Chinese would gain a much better understanding of the issues multinationals face in doing business in this country."

In the meantime, the two main Novartis business groups are in industries classified as "restricted" by the Chinese Ministry of Foreign Trade and Economic Cooperation (MOFTEC). For this reason, Novartis must typically work with Chinese joint venture partners—and multinational corporations have learned, sometimes from bitter experience, that this can bring its own challenges.

"We get a lot of support from our joint venture partners," says Barnett. "We get their interest. But regrettably their objectives are sometimes different than ours. In most cases, the Chinese partners have minority stakes, and they are usually looking for an early return on their investment. By contrast, the foreign partner is usually looking much longer-term, particularly when a large plant has been constructed. In pharmaceuticals as well as agrochemicals, economies of scale are important and it takes some time before volumes are large enough to reduce unit costs sufficiently to make the operations economically sound. Further, foreign companies in China sometimes find that feasibility studies, often carried out five years earlier on the basis of limited experience of the country, predicted positive financial performance that has taken longer in practice to materialize. When the Chinese partner discovers this, mutual trust can break down because it is typically the foreigner who prepares the business plan in the first instance. The problem gets worse still when the Chinese party, often part of a state-owned enterprise, has been given a financial forecast of significant returns from a Sino-foreign joint venture, which is in reality taking some time to achieve profitability.

"Then there is the issue of who manages the joint venture. The foreigner typically wants total control, just as he does in other countries. He considers that, having invested large sums, he is entitled to ensure that the business is managed to an international standard. On the other hand, the Chinese want significant involvement, even if they are a minority shareholder. There is the issue of 'face,' but also pride in being part of a joint venture with a large foreign enterprise. Relationships can sometimes be emotional rather than objective."

In this overall operating context, Barnett believes that when a joint venture has no chance whatever of meeting its original objectives, one must cut one's losses and sever the relationship. However, in some situations additional time must be spent with joint venture partners to find new solutions—for example, new structures such as cooperative rather than equity joint ventures, which might result in both parties' being able to achieve their different objectives. Continued focus is needed on investing in the "soft side," that is, people, systems, and training. "We have to balance the significant investment required in those areas (the knowledge areas) with the short-term need for profitability improvement."

The market environment in China is another major cause of uncertainty. Although the market is growing fast, encouraged by sustained growth in GDP, the future shape of the industries in which Novartis operates is most unclear. In the health care sector in China, traditional Chinese medicines (TCMs) have a tremendous following. It is not yet clear how medicines that have stood the test of 1000 years of successful practice will blend in with Western medicines; the latter are becoming increasingly fashionable in China, whilst not replacing TCMs. How that adaptation will work out in the end is most uncertain.

Novartis China's answer to these uncertainties is to try to get closer to the market and understand what is happening—not just in the big cities, but in rural areas as well. As Barnett stresses, "It is necessary to understand the customers' mentality and the way this is changing, to understand the information flow about your products and the way they should be promoted. Spend a lot of time talking—or rather, listening—to people."

Novartis is looking at China as a place for research and investment in research. In this way, the group hopes for a long-term relationship with the country and hopes to be considered an insider. As Barnett puts it, "Like the Chinese, we want a complete relationship, not just bricks and mortar."

Infringement of intellectual property rights has become an issue for the agrochemicals business. "If your product comes in a can or bottle," notes Barnett, "it is often possible to tell whether it is a copy, based on the quality of the packaging as well as the content. However, many agrochemicals come in a sachet that is easy to copy. When the customer puts this fake product on his crop because he has an insect or disease problem, it takes him some time to discover that it doesn't work, and even then he doesn't know why. So he comes to mistrust your product. This kills the business. The market begins to doubt the efficacy of your offering. Fortunately, we haven't experienced this phenomenon in the pharmaceuticals business yet, where the results could be much worse. For a product like Aspirin, it's one thing—but imagine if the drug being copied is a potential lifesaver. That's not so nice." To control this problem, Novartis China has been working with the PRC authorities, who share the company's concerns.

Novartis is a Swiss company with a small home market. To be successful, the company has to succeed in markets outside Switzerland. "We don't have a large home market to fall back on, as Americans and many other Europeans do," says Barnett. China represents over 20 percent of the world's population. If you are in the health care, agricultural, or nutrition businesses, that is a large market. Novartis has to succeed in China.

What are the secrets of success? I ask.

"Think short-term, but look long-term. Keep your feet firmly on the ground. This is not a country for visionaries. Maybe it was

10 years ago, but I don't think so now. I don't mean that you need to move in the lawyers, the accountants, the cost controllers. You need to improve the cost side of the equation, and that will best be done by investing more on the 'soft side'—for example, training people and localizing the business. The Chinese will understand the regulators and the markets far better than I or any other foreigner. That is, in the end, how to manage the uncertainties. That is how you succeed."

Novartis in China

Novartis operates in China through 14 different legal entities, manufacturing and marketing products in the health care, agriculture, and nutrition fields. To date, the group has invested over US$100 million in the PRC, and employs approximately 1400 people there.

8

Bridging the Gap

*The gap in trust between foreigners and
Chinese is probably the biggest gap of
all. Unless you resolve this satisfactorily,
you cannot succeed in China.*

KENT WATSON
CHAIRMAN AND COUNTRY SENIOR
PARTNER, PRICEWATERHOUSECOOPERS
CHINA LIMITED

Kent Watson has a love affair with China. It started in the mid-
1960s, when he spent three years as a missionary in Taiwan, where
he learned Mandarin and acquired a lasting interest in the language
and all things Chinese. Although he spent the next 20 years as a professional accountant with Price Waterhouse, mainly in the United
States, his hobby (as he modestly understates it) and his religious
calling took him back to Taiwan in the late 1980s. This time, he was
the head of the same Mormon mission in which he had been a
novice some 30 years earlier, and this time he was leading a flock of
some 450 missionaries.

In 1992, as the market in China began to open up for international companies, Watson was asked if he would relocate to Beijing

to head up his firm's office there. Some seven years later, following the global merger of Price Waterhouse and Coopers & Lybrand, he is now leading another flock—of accountants and business advisers. He has seen the business grow from around 50 people in 1992 to over 1200 in 1999.

As one who was born and raised in a small town in Southern Utah, Watson sometimes can hardly believe the environment and position in which he finds himself. His understanding of people, gained through his work as a missionary and as a professional accountant, together with his knowledge of China and its language, make him an ideal ambassador for PricewaterhouseCoopers and the leader of its business in China. He is able to bridge the gap between Chinese and foreigners. He is also able to bridge the expectation gap between Chinese organizations and foreign enterprises.

■ ■ ■

The story of the abortive embassy to China by King George III's representative, Lord George Macartney, is compulsory reading for those seeking an historical perspective on the failure of the West to open the Chinese market to trade in the eighteenth century. From late 1792, until he gave up in early 1794, Lord Macartney tried valiantly through diplomatic means to achieve his king's purpose. It was not to be. Emperor Qianlong had no intention of opening up the Celestial Kingdom. To make matters worse, the misunderstandings and the mistrust that developed in 1793 laid the foundation for the more direct action that the British and French shamefully took in the nineteenth century, in the name of free trade.

Many incidents gave rise to offense and misunderstanding. For example, Macartney refused to prostrate himself in a proper "kowtow," on the premise that if a simple bow was appropriate for King George, it was good enough for the Emperor. This caused great annoyance to Qianlong. The Emperor, who believed that he should accept only "tribute" from a vassal state, scorned Macartney's presentation of "gifts" from the King of England. The mixture of cultures and motives was bound to produce an explosive cocktail. To recall the Emperor's words, taken from Alain Peyrefitte's classic book, *The Collision of Two Civilisations:* "The English Barbarians have not obtained satisfaction; they are crafty and sly, and they may attempt to take revenge for their failure. We must guard against that possibility." Peyrefitte explained further: "Misunderstanding continued to deepen with each successive exchange, the Emperor pretending that he had heard Macartney say what he had not said, Macartney pretending he had not heard the Emperor say what he had."

For Watson, with his understanding of China, these words ring true of encounters some 200 years later. In his view, you quite naturally start with expectations. "Our firm in China has been involved in providing services to over 600 clients. We have, therefore, some experience of the issues involved. This cumulative experience indicates that the biggest barrier to success is the difference in expectations of the foreigners and the Chinese. Foreign investors in China of course hope for a return on their investments, but they can typically tolerate a long time frame, and the values that attract them are access to the large market and the lower cost of labor. On the other hand, Chinese joint venture partners invariably expect dividends immediately, and the values that attract them are technology and know-how, capital, and modern equipment. Bridging this expectation gap and differing values is crucial to success.

"You would think you might go about bridging that gap through an airtight negotiated agreement. If the venture has a sound business plan supported by a feasibility study, an agreed structure for governing the venture, an agreed management structure, and an agreed strategy, you would hope to achieve an overall negotiated agreement that would meet the expectations of both parties. Certainly, that is the approach you have to take. It is the prescribed approach to forming a China venture and the one that most companies actually take in starting a venture in China. But problems frequently occur afterwards because the expectations of the parties have not, in fact, been fulfilled."

Yet a foreigner and a Chinese partner may have spent a good deal of time together negotiating an agreement—one, two, even three years. After all that time, wouldn't they understand each other's expectations?

"Of course," Watson replies, "but the problem is that the people who negotiated the arrangements, on both sides of the table, are not necessarily the same people who have to make the venture successful. I frequently say that the most difficult job in the world is being the general manager of a joint venture in China. And we sometimes facetiously add that in China negotiations really only begin after the contract is signed."

It is these thoughts that lead to the next expectation gap—between the head office and local management on the ground in China. Watson continues, "On the one hand, you have the demands of the home office corporate management, who probably negotiated an agreement that they were sure would succeed. On the other hand, you have the Chinese manager and the people who negotiated the agreement for the Chinese side, who are also looking to you to make the venture successful. However, the expectations of the two sides may not necessarily be the same. Then you have the poor expatriate manager who has been seconded to China to make the whole thing work. He is in a lose/lose scenario—that is, unless he can find a way to bridge the expectation gap.

"This doesn't come about through negotiated agreements. They are less meaningful in China than in the West. Dispute settlement processes unfold differently, and they are not based upon criteria that one might consider in other jurisdictions. In my view, the gap can only be bridged when the two parties are able to build a relationship of trust. The Chinese have a saying: '*Qiu Tong Cun Yi.*' It means 'to put aside differences and seek common ground,' or 'to seek common ground while respecting differences.' I believe that to find success in China, it is necessary to adopt *Tong Cun Yi.*"

Why doesn't that trust exist? And if trust is the secret of success, how do you build it?

"To answer your first question, you need to reflect on history and also to consider the different objectives," responds Watson.

"Contact between the Chinese and the foreigner over the last 200 years has not been all that pleasant. This influences present-day attitudes. The foreigner has a wall to climb if he is to develop trust. Turning to objectives: Most multinational companies investing in China think globally. The Chinese, on the other hand, are more nationalistic. This should not come as a surprise to us. After all, they were previously isolated from the global economy. Now their motivation is to develop their economy, and they naturally want to protect their nascent industries and their own markets. This difference of objectives needs to be understood and discussed, so that mistrust is not created when doing business in this jurisdiction.

"I want to answer your second question," continues Watson, "by reference to our own activities in China. Pricewaterhouse-Coopers is in the business of providing audit, tax, and consulting services to our clients. Our global clients need us to help them develop a robust presence in China. China needs our profession—it is a profession critical to the capital formation process, critical to providing investors in China with assurance concerning the financial information on which the performance of their business and the value of their investment will be judged. It is also useful in assisting companies to deal with the many regulatory issues, some would say red tape, that might be restrictive or certainly inhibit innovation and productivity.

"Because our profession did not exist in China for 40 years, there is no qualified pool of local professionals to provide the services needed. To make up for this, we have a much higher ratio of expatriates to local staff than any other foreign business I am aware of in China. Our focus, therefore, is on training and developing our people. Training is not just for purposes of increasing efficiency and production. It will also create equals. We want to develop people who will become true partners, with the same capability to provide professional services to global clients that a skilled expatriate might have. So, you see, we are attempting to develop a relationship of trust with our Chinese partners and our local staff. We want them to become the leaders of our business in the future. This is the message we have to get across—and we have to live that message.

"Another Chinese saying comes to mind, namely '*Xiang De Yi Zhang*,*'* which means 'each shining more brilliantly in the other's company,' or 'to bring out the best in each other.' I would hope that in China our efforts will result in a *Xiang De Yi Zhang* relationship."

Training and localization are common themes for foreign businesses in China. How does this differ, if at all, in building the business of PricewaterhouseCoopers in China?

"We have a four-point program," responds Watson. "First, we strive to hire the brightest and best graduates from the top universities in China. Second, we have established a training center in Shanghai. When staff members join us, they are subject to a rigorous 12-week training program so that they can learn our culture and obtain foundation skills in the profession. Our objective is for each of them to become a certified public accountant as soon as possible. We are succeeding in this respect, as our staff applicants achieve a pass rate on individual papers in China's CPA examinations of 40 percent, versus the national average of 10 percent. We also provide, annually, 40 to 80 hours of additional classroom training in our training center for each member of our staff.

"However, the most important training we provide is on the job. Each staff member is assigned a mentor whose responsibility it is to transfer knowledge and skills, so that our staff have the opportunity not only to become proficient at their work but also to become the managers and team leaders of the future. And finally—point four—we have our overseas development program. I'm not given to exaggeration, but this is quite awesome. Each member of our staff with a few years of experience has the opportunity of a two-year overseas assignment. The objective is for them to become proficient in a second language and better understand the global nature of our business. We are currently providing this opportunity to approximately 100 staff members each year. In addition, we have 50 members of our staff who are now studying for advanced degrees in overseas universities."

Watson believes that the PricewaterhouseCoopers concept of training is distinctive, in the sense that rather than training staff to develop specific skills, his firm trains staff to become managers and then partners, equipped with skills applicable worldwide. In his view, this is how you build a relationship of trust.

Further, he believes that expatriates who are seconded to China have a dual responsibility—first, to provide outstanding service to PricewaterhouseCoopers clients, and second, to mentor and to build true partnerships with the firm's PRC staff. This brings him to another subject, in which his views have clearly been influenced by his six years in Taiwan. As it turned out, those years were excellent preparation for his present role in China. He believes that expatriates who come to China speaking Mandarin have a far better chance of bridging the gap.

Watson continues, "Naturally I have a bias because of my background. But it seems to me that there are three types of expatriates in China. The first type comes for a fixed term, say three years, as part of a career plan. Ensuring the long-term success of the venture through developing a lasting relationship with the Chinese partner is not and cannot be high on that person's agenda. The second type comes sometimes for longer and does an outstanding job for the company he or she represents, but lives essentially within the expatriate community. This type often expects China to be much like the home country—but ethnocentrism of that kind can mislead this individual into becoming quite critical. No relationship of trust is likely to develop. The third type tries to be more involved in the Chinese environment. I would say that people who have an interest in the language, people who are sensitive to cultural differences, people who get beyond their expatriate world, are far more effective in accomplishing what needs to be done in building trust between the local and foreign partners."

For Watson, the ability to speak Mandarin is a key success factor. He does not believe that expatriates can be effective in developing the right relationships unless they can relate to Chinese staff in their own language. On the subject of relationships or *guanxi,* Watson has a seasoned viewpoint. "Many foreigners refer to the importance of relationships in China in terms of *guanxi.* They somehow have the impression that *guanxi* means giving favors and thereby being owed favors. I don't view it that way. I view *guanxi* more in terms of sincerity. What Pricewaterhouse-Coopers is trying to do as a firm in China is to actually provide an opportunity for our Chinese staff to become equals as partners in a global organization, sharing the same rewards on the same basis. That, to me, is what real *guanxi* is all about. If we can get this right, then we will bridge the gap, both in terms of expectation and in terms of trust. Then we'll have developed a successful long-term business in China."

PricewaterhouseCoopers in China

PricewaterhouseCoopers has origins in China dating back to 1903, through one of its legacy firms. After the Open Door policy was announced in 1978 and Western companies began establishing operations in the PRC, both Coopers & Lybrand and Price Waterhouse opened representative offices in 1981. As investment increased in the early 1990s, the two firms, which merged internationally in July 1998, began to increase their resources in response to client needs. There was a growing demand for advisory and audit services from international companies in China and from domestic companies seeking foreign equity finance.

Today, PricewaterhouseCoopers China has offices in Beijing, Dalian, Guangzhou, Shanghai, and Shenzhen, with over 1200 people working on the mainland. An additional 3000 Chinese speakers work for the firm in Hong Kong and Taiwan.

PricewaterhouseCoopers China experiences demand from multinational corporations for its services in the following areas:

- *Market entry*—strategic planning, business advice, registration, negotiation, transaction services, tax planning, and completion audit
- *Cost reduction and process improvement*—tax and regulatory advice, supply chain management, financial and cost man-

agement, introduction of ERP systems (including SAP and Oracle), and internal audit

- *Regulatory services*—tax compliance, statutory audit, international financial reporting, and labor compliance

Additional services provided to Chinese enterprises include acting as reporting accountants on overseas share issues and stock exchange listings, business advice, and statutory audit services.

9

The Banner
and the Reality

*Most people follow the banner. Before I
came to China, I was influenced by what
I read. Now that I'm here, I see the
reality—and it's very different.*
BRIAN ANDERSON
CHAIRMAN & CHIEF EXECUTIVE,
SHELL COMPANIES IN NORTH
EAST ASIA

Brian Anderson of Shell is based in Beijing, although his bailiwick
extends to Korea, Taiwan, and the Hong Kong SAR, as well as the
mainland. He took up his position in late 1997, starting with a six-
week course in Mandarin, after spending the previous three and a
half years as managing director of Shell in Nigeria.

Anderson's previous posting was like going home, since he was
born and spent his childhood in Nigeria, where his father worked
for 47 years as a mining engineer. He grew up in a very quiet bush
environment, where the local people lived a marginal existence in
mud huts. With the initial intention of following in his father's
footsteps, Anderson graduated from Camborne School of Mining
in Cornwall and worked in Nigeria until civil war intervened.
After studying petroleum engineering at London University's

Royal School of Mines, he joined Shell in 1968 and was posted to Norway; subsequent assignments took him to Brunei, the Netherlands, Oman, Australia (twice), Malaysia (three different postings), and finally Nigeria and China.

He has many passions; one of these, sailing, led to his resignation from Shell in 1973 to embark on a six-month voyage from the UK to the West African coast. He had wanted a leave of absence, but it wasn't granted. In the end, Anderson took nine months off—and returned to Shell with a better job and with his Japanese wife-to-be, whom he had met while in Switzerland studying French. In addition to speaking English, French, and Dutch, he possesses basic linguistic abilities in Mandarin, Japanese, and Hausa.

Anderson points out that, although a British passport holder, he has never worked in the UK in his 30-year career. Because he is not linked to any particular country, he feels very much part of the country in which he currently happens to be posted by Shell. Perhaps for this reason, he is a man who likes to make a contribution to the countries in which he works. This was recognized in Malaysia, where he was made a Datuk by the State of Sabah, and also by the State of Sarawak.

■ ■ ■

Of all the challenges facing the head of China's leading international oil company, Brian Anderson particularly focuses on three issues:

- How do I get a better handle on the evolving and changing market?
- How can I reduce costs?
- How can I get people to differentiate between the banner and the reality?

Anderson becomes most passionate concerning the third issue, perhaps because in his previous job he had to contend with international press criticism of Shell's role in Nigeria at a time when the country was being accused of human rights violations. Perhaps it is because he has no real roots and has become, quite literally, a citizen of the world, with few prejudices and few preconceived ideas about the new situations in which he finds himself. Or perhaps it is because his maxim for getting on in Asia is "Shut up and listen."

"Before I came to China," Anderson begins, "I had read that China was different. What surprised me is that it was different in ways I didn't expect, and some of the differences I had read about were misconceptions. For example, you read a lot about human rights, coercive government, and the rights of the individual. But China is more liberal than I expected. Although the market is restricted, it is still much more open than, say, Korea. Contrary to what I had read, there is no special antipathy toward foreigners, just a natural desire to make money through business relationships. This happens all over the world. It's perfectly normal."

With a Japanese wife and almost half of his career spent in Asia, Anderson has much to say about the secrets of business success in Asia. "The fundamental thing is that you must have respect for each other. It is really that simple. When you are dealing with people, you can be very frank and very direct. But for it to work, they have to believe that you are sincere, and to achieve this you have to develop a good, but simple, relationship. This isn't about wining and dining—it's much more fundamental. If you genuinely become part of a country and part of a system without abdicating your principles, then you'll go a long way. We try very hard at Shell to do this." This concept of partnership with local governments is one that stems from the group's history. Oil can be a very political business. While Shell tries to be apolitical, it also seeks to maintain good relations with the governments and the countries in which the group operates. In Royal Dutch, for example, a favorite maxim was the Dutch proverb "Cooperation gives strength." Further, in the Statement of General Business Principles that guides the governance of each of the Royal Dutch/Shell companies, emphasis is placed on the contribution that Shell can make to the social and material progress of countries in which the group operates.

■ ■ ■

Although Shell was founded by Europeans, its origins lie in Asia and date back to nineteenth-century international trade there. One of the founding entities, the predecessor to Shell Transport & Trading Company, imported Russian kerosene into China in 1891 and built storage sites, with associated can-making plants, in Shanghai and Hong Kong. The other founding company, Royal Dutch, began exporting its rival "Crown" kerosene from the Dutch East Indies to China in 1894. Over the next decade, both companies developed facilities for shipping oil to key Chinese cities, including Guangzhou, Hankou, Shantou, Tianjin, and Xiamen.

In 1903, the two companies formed a joint marketing company, together with the Paris branch of the Rothschild family, which had oil interests in Russia. This gave birth to the Asiatic Petroleum Company (APC), a precursor to the full amalgamation in 1907, of Royal Dutch and Shell Transport. Better able to fight off competition from the American giants such as Standard Oil Company, APC expanded fast in China and soon acquired premises in Shanghai with the prestigious address of Number 1, The Bund (later renamed The Asiatic Building). By 1939, APC had almost 400,000 tons of tankage in China, with major installations in Shanghai, Hankou, Tianjin, Guangzhou, Qingdao, and Nanjing. The group had 1000 sales outlets across 20 provinces.

Following the outbreak of the Second World War, APC's possessions in China and Hong Kong were seized by the invading Japanese forces. The subsequent fighting caused untold damage. By 1945, less than 10 percent of APC's prewar capacity remained. Sixty percent of the tanker fleet had been destroyed and all of the company's motor vehicles were missing. But Shell's commitment to the China market was demonstrated when, starting in 1946, the corporation began to rebuild its activities in Hong Kong and the mainland. Even after 1949, when the American oil companies withdrew and APC's business was again requisitioned, Shell remained and became the only Western oil company trading in China. Regrettably, as the years passed, the trading environment deteriorated and Shell was obliged to withdraw from the country completely in 1966, at the onset of the Cultural Revolution.

Allowed back in 1980, the group's China representative was soon permitted to rent a disused building in the Summer Palace, known as the Clouds Gathering Pavilion. Fortunately, a new storm did not materialize and the operating environment gradually became more friendly. In 1983, partnerships were formed for oil exploration ventures in the South China Sea. In 1985, again showing its commitment to the China market, Shell established a fuels depot at Shekou, near Shenzhen. This was followed in 1991 by an agreement to develop the Xijiang oil field, some 150 kilometers south of Hong Kong, jointly with the China National Offshore Oil Corporation (CNOOC) and Phillips, the operator. Shell today is the largest international equity producer of oil in China.

■ ■ ■

The group has investments in mainland China, now totalling US$1 billion, which include:

- Establishment of joint ventures in many provinces for the storage, transportation, and marketing of fuels, liquified petroleum gas (LPG), bitumen, and lubricants
- Exploration in the Liaohe oilfield in Liaoning Province
- Assessment of the economic viability of gas from the Ordos Basin in Shaanxi Province

Looking forward, Shell's largest and most important future investment in China is the Nanhai project to build a US$4.5 billion petrochemicals complex near Huizhou, in Guangdong Province, which will produce ethylene and derivative products. At a time when the group is shutting down or selling off 40 percent of its worldwide chemicals portfolio, Shell considers China to be a key market where it wants to establish a leading position.

Another area of great interest to Shell is liquified natural gas (LNG), which can be imported into China and is economically and environmentally preferable to existing energy sources, both for power generation and for use as domestic gas.

The other interesting business prospect is coal gasification. China has huge reserves of coal, which will remain the primary energy source for decades to come. Turning coal into synthesis gas, for the production of fertilizer and for power, will help significantly to reduce pollution in a country where this has become a major environmental and health concern.

The historical and current developments described in the previous paragraphs demonstrate the group's consistent focus on China over a period of more than a century. They also help to explain some of the behavioral characteristics of decision making within Shell. As Anderson puts it, "APC was effectively a Chinese company. In the early days, when the General Manager in Shanghai wanted to communicate with London, he couldn't simply pick up the phone. Messages were sent by steamship. The issues he faced were complex, and they were local. So the General Manager ran his business as he felt it should be run, with little guidance from the center. This influenced his thinking and behavior. It made him focus exclusively on the national market he had to serve."

■ ■ ■

"The biggest problem I have," Anderson explains, "is getting a handle on the marketplace. All the rest is relatively straightforward for a company like Shell that operates in most countries around the world. This is a reentry to an existing market. Matching our investment in China to the growth in the market is a tricky game. This is the issue that consumes us most of the time. In an old-fashioned world, the process of new investment would take longer. Today's world doesn't allow that. You just have to go faster.

"Of the US$1 billion we have invested in China in the last 15 years, US$600 million has been spent in exploration and production. We are the largest foreign equity oil producer in China. That sounds grandiose. In fact, at only 40,000 barrels a day, it's very small. We have an equity share of only about 1 percent of China's oil production. This shows you that the PRC Government hasn't really opened up the oil industry. We have been very cautious about investing in this sector because there have been a lot of burnt fingers as a result of oil companies' going into marginal areas and struggling to make them viable. We are profitable—and one of the few who can say that.

"In oil products and chemicals, we have just finished our first cycle of investment of around US$300 million. It's been a patchy start. Some projects have worked better than others. None is profitable at the moment. But they are all very recent, built within the last two years. We expect them to come to profitability within the next two years. Oil products are a restrictive game in China. The PRC government withdrew the right from us to go into the retail market for fuels like petrol and diesel, which provide a shop front for oil companies. You will nevertheless see some Shell petrol stations. They stem from a grandfather clause in the legislation, which allows us to use the arrangements that existed before the rules were changed. So, by the end of 1998, we had about 30 filling stations. We also sell lubricants and, at a much smaller level, some bitumen and LPG.

"You will hear from everyone that in our industry the market in China is difficult. Normally, in a new market, we would import our products and test the market out first. If the circumstances and financial projections looked right, we would then invest and build capacity. Here in China, that's not possible. You have to invest up front—and that's a killer. There is a further problem: overcapacity being built in China at present because of overinvestment. This is particularly bad in lubricants and LPG. As a result, there is going to be rationalization of capacity in the next few years. Additionally, Chinese competition is strong, and the rules of the game are unclear. It's a battle, but I'm optimistic because the country is led by some very smart people and the market will eventually sort itself out."

■ ■ ■

The third subject that concerns Anderson is the high cost of employing expatriates in China. "The only way we can work out the market and make it work for us is to employ the best people. We have some great local hires who are of high quality and young, but they are very inexperienced. To get over this, we need to fill the gap with very expensive foreigners. Cost is a big issue, and I think the PRC Government should do something to help reduce it. When these costs are kept high, the transfer of knowledge is probably slower than it should be. Add to this the length of time required to obtain approvals and deal with complex and ever-changing regulations. Since these often involve the costly foreigner, there is a very strong disincentive to invest."

These are issues that affect every multinational company doing business in China—but, in the oil industry, because of its importance to the economy and the size of investment needed, the problems are on a grander scale.

■ ■ ■

This brings Anderson back to his theme of getting the right message across. "An important consideration is to ensure that there are realistic expectations back home. It's important to ensure that your shareholders understand China and the processes you have to go through. It's also important to get the right message across to the authorities in China.

"If we develop the right relationship with the government of a country, we can have frank and open dialogue. And this is how we can make a difference. Shell helps countries earn money. We work with countries to generate wealth for the people. I have a deep personal interest in helping countries, particularly those in the developing world. My core belief is that I can help create and find solutions both for Shell and for the country in which the group operates. It's not just a commercial game. But, to achieve results, you have to strip away the veneer. You have to deal with the facts and face them honestly. So far as China is concerned, apart from being a realist, I am an optimist—provided that you can get behind the banner."

Shell in China

Shell is the leading international oil company operating in China. With an investment in the last 15 years of some US$1 billion, it employs over 1000 people and has an annual turnover of US$400 million. Through its 20 wholly owned or joint venture operations, Shell is involved in a wide range of oil, gas, and chemicals projects and activities. These include exploration and production, oil processing and trading, oil marketing, chemicals, natural gas, coal imports and coal gasification, power generation, and the development of renewable energy.

10

Twenty-First-Century Comprador

Esse Quam Videri (To be, rather than to seem to be)
JIM CONYBEARE
DIRECTOR, JOHN SWIRE & SONS

John Swire established his trading business in Liverpool in 1816. The Napoleonic Wars had just ended and England's victory had opened up the world's trading routes. The company's focus was Asia, and its first operating office in China was established in Shanghai in 1866. Thus began the development of a tradition and knowledge base that have led to the Swire Group's becoming a favored partner for many international companies wishing to do business on the Chinese mainland.

The company's motto, *Esse Quam Videri*, reflects the founder's Yorkshire origins: You are judged on performance, rather than on image. This corporate philosophy has been carried down over the years and imbues personnel and company procedures. For example, in the corporate policy for reimbursement of personal expenses incurred on company business, there are no detailed rules, just the simple injunction: "Expenses shall be claimed unproudly." Although "unproudly" does not appear in the *Oxford English Dictionary* or in *Webster's,* everyone in the Group knows what it means.

Jim Conybeare is an embodiment of Swire traditions, and his qualifications as a modern-day comprador are difficult to match. He has spent his entire career in Asia, starting in Hong Kong in 1967 as a second officer with Swire's shipping arm, the China Navigation Company, and he is in the most literal sense wedded to Asia. In 1969, he married Miki, who is Japanese, and there is, as he puts it, "a good understanding of Asia around the home."

Conybeare has worked in Hong Kong, Papua New Guinea, Taiwan, and Singapore. For four years, from the end of 1988, he was the Swire Group's Chairman in Taiwan, after which, in March 1993, he took on his present responsibility for Swire Pacific's Industries Division, playing a major part in developing the Group's activities in China. When asked what has given him most pride in this role, his reply is modest, in keeping with both the Swire Group's corporate ethos and his own Asian experience: "We try to do everything to the best of our ability."

■ ■ ■

Jim Conybeare's modesty belies the success Swire has enjoyed to date in mainland China, establishing no fewer than 21 joint ventures with some of the world's leading companies, including Coca-Cola, Carlsberg, Crown Cork & Seal, Groupe Schneider, ICI, and Tate & Lyle. This success is underlined by the fact that most of the joint venture operations have been established on time and to budget—and further verified by such statistics as a Coca-Cola sales growth in excess of 22 percent in 1998.

Most of Swire's manufacturing activities on the mainland have been established during the last six years, after Conybeare took over responsibility for Swire's Beverages and Industrial operations. At times, as Conybeare admits, he and his staff were negotiating on too many fronts simultaneously, and this led to some problems with contracts and joint venture partners, but none so grave as to be regarded with hindsight as major stumbling blocks. To date, Swire is still with the same foreign and PRC partners, and none of the joint ventures has been terminated.

Conybeare stresses that his experience in Taiwan was invaluable in equipping him for the role he now plays on the mainland. He has lived in Taiwan on two separate occasions during his 32-year career with Swire in Asia. He recalls that during his first visit to Keelung, in February 1967, he received some memorable advice from Swire's then Taiwan shipping agent, Dawson Kwauk: "Jim, I think you'll be coming here quite a lot, so let me give you some advice. You must remember one thing so that you can survive in Asia. When we Chinese say 'Yes,' we don't mean 'Yes, we will do it.' We don't mean 'Yes, we understand.' All we mean is, 'Yes, we heard you say something.' As long as you can remember that, you will be successful."

Understanding each other is a recurrent theme in Conybeare's analysis of the reasons behind successful joint ventures in China. "I can't overemphasize the importance of having a good interpreter," he says. "It's vital to have someone who doesn't just understand the words, but the nuances as well—someone who knows the business and understands what both sides hope to gain from the partnership. That way, you can begin to put yourself in the shoes of your main-land partners and work toward common goals.

"I was lucky. A colleague whom I first met in Taiwan has worked with me in putting our messages across to our mainland joint venture partners. Great patience is required to build up the necessary level of trust and you mustn't rush it, particularly when you are trying to acquire a substantial interest in a state-controlled business. One of our most successful joint ventures today is our Coca-Cola franchise in Guangdong Province. That took three years to negotiate, and, after all that time, we got to know each other pretty well. As a result, we have an excellent relationship at board level.

"Understanding the way mainland bureaucracy works is key. I must say, very pointedly, that it's a Chinese and not a Communist bureaucracy. The bureaucracy on the mainland is in some ways not dissimilar to that which I experienced in Taiwan. You have to get the same number of chops [official seals]; there is the same need for relationship building on various different levels. On the mainland, it is particularly important that you understand where authority is vested at central, provincial, and municipal levels. And you must observe the correct protocol: You must know the level of any particular individual with whom you are dealing, so that you don't embarrass him by asking for something that is not within his authority and put him in a position where he has to refuse."

Some PRC joint ventures complain about the cost of technology and the cost of expatriates who are the conduits of that technology. Once again, Conybeare believes that trust is the key. "My experience is that you must be able to show the Chinese partner that you can add value to the business. Then he will ultimately agree to an appropriate level of remuneration and to the cost of the technology. In the early days, this took time and patience, but it's getting easier all the time. This is partially because we can point to the successful joint ventures we've established in the past and demonstrate the ways in which we can add value, but it's also because mainlanders are now much more tuned in to Western ways of doing business. They know that when they're producing an internationally recognized product, such as Coca-Cola or Carlsberg, achieving a uniform quality standard is absolutely vital and that this means investing in technology and know-how."

As businesses in China expand their activities, there is, as everywhere else, a need to retain or inject funds as working capital or to increase capacity. In the old days, foreign investors sometimes found it difficult to explain this to their Chinese partners because they believed that their partners would invariably want quick and consistent returns. However, Conybeare has found his mainland counterparts increasingly appreciative of economic realities. "Of course, you must not promise a level of dividend income and then suddenly try to switch it off because you need to invest more capital. It's very important to work with your partners on a no-surprise basis, so that when you need to expand capacity they know the implications." There is a need to ensure that all local and foreign shareholders recognize that most business ventures need long-term commitments and reinvestment to grow the business. This is particularly relevant because the mainland import duty concessions in the mid-1990s encouraged the development of surplus capacity in many manufacturing businesses. In other words, it takes time to achieve remittable profits.

An understanding of the mainland business environment has led Conybeare to focus on the introduction of reward systems. "Workers from state-owned factories are loyal to the Party or the state. When you participate in a business in China, you also have to convince them to be loyal to the company you have established—not to you as the foreign partner, nor to the local Chinese partner, but to the business itself. This requires a proper payroll and reward system, so that you can identify the people who do a good job and reward them accordingly."

Swires has an extensive training program for PRC employees. At Taikoo (Xiamen) Aircraft Engineering Company (TAECO), the Group's aircraft engineering joint venture at Xiamen, during the last five years more than 500 apprentices have been seconded to Hong Kong for two or more years of training. This venture is jointly owned by Hong Kong Aircraft Engineering (HAECO), Cathay Pacific Airways, Singapore Airlines, Japanese Airlines, and Boeing, together with both local Xiamen and Beijing development partners. TAECO's aircraft engineers are certified not only by the CAAC in China, but by the U.S. Federal Aviation Authority and the UK Civil Aviation Department. As Conybeare notes, "You and I have to be comfortable that when our engineers say that a plane is in good condition to fly, they mean it and they're qualified to say so."

In the first quarter of 1999, Swire Beverages put no fewer than 1200 PRC nationals through the Group's sales training program. For the Coca-Cola joint ventures alone, some 60 graduates will be recruited this year and sent on to the graduate training program. "One of the pieces of advice I would give a potential successor," says Conybeare, "is the importance of training—of both expatriates and locals."

Swire's business in mainland China has developed as a natural extension of the Group's business activities, and in some cases its relationships, in Hong Kong. For example, the Group's relationship with Coca-Cola in Hong Kong dates back to 1965, and Swire sold its first consignment of Coca-Cola to the mainland market in 1979. With ICI, the relationship began in the 1980s when both companies had paint factories in Hong Kong, which were merged and the businesses rationalized. The two are now partners in two paint production facilities on the mainland. Swire had also been in partnership with Crown Cork & Seal for more than 20 years, before the two established their first joint venture in mainland China to produce aluminum beverage cans. A Swire subsidiary, Taikoo Sugar, had been producing sugar products in Hong Kong since 1884, before joining forces with Tate & Lyle on the mainland. Other companies, such as Groupe Schneider, were attracted to Swire as a partner in China because of the Group's knowledge of the market and business environment.

"We were looking for blue-chip partners, and some blue-chip partners were looking for opportunities to invest in China but lacked the total confidence to do so," says Conybeare. "In this respect, we acted something like a latter-day comprador, as we were the ones on the ground with knowledge and a proven history. We worked with other foreign companies and made them comfortable as we developed businesses together in China, and put significant equity into these businesses so that we could actively participate. In this respect also, we acted like nineteenth-century compradors, who often staked their own capital and reputations on the success of the foreign ventures for which they acted."

For Swire Pacific, the role of modern comprador is paying off.

The Swire Group in Mainland China

Swire has a number of significant trading and industrial activities in mainland China, held principally through Swire Pacific's Industries Division, which also has interests in Hong Kong, Taiwan, and the United States. Although the group had businesses on the mainland in the nineteenth century, these ceased in the early 1950s, after the Revolution. Trading activities recommenced in the early 1980s.

Swire's first manufacturing businesses in the PRC were established with The Coca-Cola Company in Hangzhou and Nanjing in 1988. Since then, six other Sino-foreign joint ventures have been formed with Coca-Cola in Guangzhou, Xiamen, Xian, Zhengzhou, Hefei, and Dongguan. These operations bottle Western brands such as Coca-Cola, Sprite, and Fanta, as well as soft drinks designed specifically for the local market, such as Tian Yu Di ("Heaven and Earth") and Smart. In each case, there is a local Chinese partner and, in most cases, also a national partner or partners. The national partner may be China International Trust and Investment Corporation (CITIC), with which Swire's partnership goes back to 1985, or China National Cereals, Oils and Foodstuffs Import and Export Corporation (COFCO); in some businesses both participate. Swire Coca-Cola has more than 54 sales locations in the PRC.

Swire's industrial joint ventures include operations with Crown Cork & Seal (aluminum cans), Groupe Schneider (electric bus ducts), ICI (paints), Tate & Lyle (sugar), Carlsberg (beer), and various local partners. Together with Carlsberg, Swire Pacific operates breweries in Huizhou and Shanghai. Other Swire interests in China include a number of aircraft engineering joint ventures, administrative and data processing services, property development, and travel agency services. Swire Pacific's Trading Division holds franchises in mainland China for a number of internationally known brands, including Volvo automobiles and Reebok sports shoes.

Turnover for Swire Pacific's various businesses on the mainland during 1998 amounted to US$300 million.

11

Clever and
Sensible
Adaptation
Is Key

*With 1.2 billion mouths to feed and
2.4 billion armpits to wash, China is
a huge consumer market, requiring
local product offerings and tailored
communications to reach that market.*
BRUNO LEMAGNE
PRESIDENT, UNILEVER CHINA GROUP

With international roots dating back to the latter part of the nineteenth century, Unilever has a reputation for taking global brands
and making them local successes in the many countries where it
operates. At the time of writing, Unilever China manufactures
products as varied as detergent, soap, shampoo, face cream, soy
sauce, tea, and ice cream, and Unilever regards China as a key geographical market for its consumer products.

Recognizing the importance of the market in the Greater Shanghai area around the Yangtse River Basin, including the high per-capita income earning provinces of Zhejiang and Jiangsu, Unilever based its senior China Group management team (covering China, Taiwan, and Hong Kong) in Shanghai. Located on the 14th floor of a modern building, Unilever's Shanghai premises are close to the market and as technologically advanced as any in the world.

Bruno Lemagne has been with Unilever for 28 years. Much of this time has been in Europe. He came to Shanghai in 1997. As a Belgian who has worked with the group in the UK, he has observed the impact of different cultures and different languages on business life. In his view, the differences in the operating environment in China are pronounced, but they do not have as much strategic impact as is popularly imagined.

■ ■ ■

"So much is distinctive about China," notes Lemagne. "Its size and scale, its history, the varied customs and behaviors of its people. China is different, but the strategic issues are not all that different from those encountered in other developing markets. Implementation must, however, be compatible with Chinese experience and traditions. Look at 'loss of face'. Are there many people who would like to lose face? This is not particularly a Chinese issue. However, the way it is dealt with, the way it is interpreted, is very Chinese. The implementation is different. Adaptation is what it's all about."

Bruno Lemagne puts a new spin on the received wisdom that China is a market unlike any other, where the business environment, regulatory framework, and culture are so different that special strategies are required to compete effectively. In Lemagne's opinion, the differences apparent in doing business in China are also present in most markets of the world. Six areas stand out for particular comment:

- Product offerings
- Human capital
- Marketing and communications
- Logistics
- The legal environment
- Competition

"China is the largest consumer market in the world," observes Lemagne. "With 1.2 billion mouths to feed and 2.4 billion armpits to wash, China represents huge potential for Unilever with its wide varieties of consumer products." However, based on its present range of Western product offerings, Lemagne believes that Unilever's products are only capable of reaching 10 to 12 percent of the total market. There is a need to adapt the product offerings so that they appeal to the Chinese consumer. Some products, such as Coca-Cola, McDonalds, and Lipton, can be truly global. But most consumer products require tailoring. They cannot be taken lock, stock, and barrel off the shelf and transported to the supermarkets of Beijing and the shops of Nanjing. "Wall's ice cream is well-known in many countries," comments Lemagne, "but its flavors vary region by region, based on local taste and local culinary history. In the West, for example, people like their ice cream to contain a lot of dairy and a lot of sugar. Not so in China, where neither features in the Chinese diet. Tastes are different. It is more likely, then, that the next ice cream flavor in China will not be mint chocolate chip or tiramisu, but red bean." Unilever's published purpose of being a multilocal multinational applies as much to China as to the 100 other countries in which the group operates.

"I lived in the UK for a number of years," says Lemagne. "Therefore, when I receive a letter from the head office, I can understand what it means. But if I only had a book knowledge of English, I would not always understand. The English and Americans are totally different from each other in their behavior and their uses of their common language. But they have learned to understand and communicate with each other to make their business contacts effective and productive. China is different again, and in a different way. We have to learn to adapt." For Unilever, this means trying to create an environment in the company where people speak their minds—something that does not come naturally in China.

More important, it means an emphasis on localization. Lemagne finds it difficult to imagine that a marketing or brand manager can be truly effective if he does not have the full information about a market that can typically best be gathered and understood by a local. Localization plugs you into the local environment and ensures that the distinctive features of the Chinese market are more fully understood. Having fewer expatriates is a bonus, but not a reason in itself for greater localization. As Lemagne puts it, "Our operations in Germany are Unilever operations with a distinctive German focus. China will develop in the same way."

If communicating between people of different nations has its complications, then communicating with consumer markets in different countries has its own complications as well. Lemagne points to the use in UK advertisements of British humor, which may be totally misunderstood by Continental European audiences. For example, Unilever's advertisements in the UK for its PG Tips tea products used to feature chimpanzees—something that Continental Europeans could not possibly understand. The Chinese, by comparison, take most things at face value. You mustn't be clever or funny. It is so easy to miscommunicate or offend. Thus, while the channels for reaching and influencing consumer audiences may be the same, the message content and strategy need adaptation to succeed. In China, there are billboards, television, consumer magazines. But it's not just the Chinese characters that are different in the advertisements, it's the messages themselves and the way they are communicated.

Multinational corporations doing business in China bemoan the lack of an efficient national, as well as local, distribution and warehousing industry. Traditionally, Chinese manufacturers had their own distribution capabilities and supplied mainly to local customers. Typically, foreign companies must in the first instance develop their own logistics. For Unilever, this is nothing new. When

Unilever first entered the ice cream market in Europe some 50 years ago, there was no available distribution system for the product. Unilever had to develop its own, including warehousing and trucking capabilities. With such experiences still vivid in Unilever's institutional memory, Lemagne is not despondent. "China builds every year the equivalent of the existing motorway system of the Benelux countries—and you cannot say that Belgium and Holland are not well provided with motorways. There is one linking every two villages; the system is very impressive. We need to adapt in China, just as we have in other countries."

"I am very bullish about China," continues Lemagne. "Look at what has already happened: command economy to market economy; rural to urban; tackling the problems of the SOEs (State-Owned Enterprises) and the banks; the infrastructure developments. The country is being professionally managed."

But it's the legal framework that causes Lemagne to spend the longest time explaining the difficulties. "The Chinese have made some amazing changes in the last 20 years, but the legal system has yet to catch up. There are laws, but these are not always clear, and they are not always necessarily enforced equally. The protection of intellectual property rights is a big issue. There is smuggling of 'grays' (gray market goods) and copying. It's bad enough that copying your products takes business away from you. But, worse still, it cheats customers and destroys the company's image and brands that have been painstakingly built up over decades. This is a major problem for a company such as Unilever that relies on developing its brands. The group in China has established a special department to follow up and attempt to deal with infringements. While there is full collaboration from the central government in Beijing, some local authorities are not always supportive, perhaps due to local protectionism, and fines are an insufficient deterrent."

By comparison, in other countries a legal judgment can be obtained against an infringement within 72 hours. But even on this subject, Lemagne is philosophical. "This used to be a big issue for us in Singapore 20 years ago. Now there's no problem. And on protectionism, what country doesn't practice it in some way? China will quickly come to the conclusion that protectionism doesn't work in the long run. Businesses survive by efficiently meeting the needs of their customers and consumers. Operating in China has its peculiarities and frustrations, but the opportunities outweigh the problems."

It's not just intellectual property rights that are adversely affected by the nascent legal environment, but also financial assets. In Unilever's experience, the time period for the collection of debts is worse in China than in most other countries. Enforcing judgments against debtors in the PRC is not straightforward and makes credit risk assessment and other credit control measures key objectives for most financial controllers.

One other problem for multinationals operating in China, particularly consumer products companies, is the intensity of competition. So great has it been that in 1998 prices in some sectors have fallen. Some multinationals have thrown in the towel and left the country. Concentration is already taking place at the local level, encouraged by the government's policy of "Let the Big survive." But despite these changes, the market in China resembles those of Europe or the United States 50 years ago, when industries were fragmented and dozens of companies manufactured cars, typewriters, airplanes, and other products. As Lemagne puts it, "In those days, there was a margarine manufacturer in every village. Now, only the largest companies have survived."

"Today, in Europe, you have European, some American, and a few Japanese competitors. In Japan, you have Japanese, some American, and a few European competitors. In the United States, you have American, some European, and a few Japanese competitors. But in China, everyone is here. In addition, you have very serious local competitors and they are getting stronger. The competitive pressure will not go away. It does not frighten us. However, it doesn't make life easy."

"So what do you have to do to succeed?" I ask.

"You have to be better at creating a local business. To be successful in China, Unilever needs to be a Chinese company and serve the Chinese market—with all the support of a global organization. Adapt better to the local environment, and you'll win."

Unilever in China

Unilever has 13 operating entities and a holding company in China. Its main product groups comprise food (ice cream, tea, and culinary products) and home and personal care needs (detergents, personal wash, hair, and skin products, and toothpaste). Unilever's main operations on the mainland are in Beijing, Shanghai, Guangzhou, and Hefei.

12

Looking at the Problem through Chinese Eyes

When a Western factory manager comes to China, he tries to re-create the factory he knew back home. With hard work and perseverance he can change the walls, the floors, the machinery, and the product. What he cannot easily change are the expectations of the employees about their relationships with their Chinese managers.
DR. RICHARD LATHAM
PRESIDENT, UNITED TECHNOLOGIES
INTERNATIONAL—CHINA

Richard Latham has been involved with China for over 30 years, more than half of which have been spent in Asia. His views on Chinese society, culture, and business practices are therefore based on greater knowledge and experience than are likely to be possessed by most Westerners who head multinational corporations in China.

Latham's involvement in China started at Brigham Young University in the United States in the mid-1960s, when he studied Chinese. This was followed by a spell in Taiwan, where his linguistic skills were enhanced. (He is now fluent in Mandarin.) As a U.S. Air Force officer, he had another spell in Taiwan and served two tours in Hong Kong. He was the first U.S. military officer to lecture in Chinese at the Chinese Academy of Social Sciences. In the early 1980s, he also undertook research at Beijing University.

After obtaining a Ph.D. at the University of Washington, Latham became interested in management, and in the early 1990s he led the U.S. Air Force Total Quality Management initiative in the Washington, D.C., area (an initiative that included the Air Staff in the Pentagon). In 1992, Latham took the leap: He left the U.S. Air Force as a colonel, and joined United Technologies Corporation (UTC) with the objective of going to China.

Since then, apart from leading UTC in the PRC, he has lectured widely and written a number of works on China, including a book on Chinese and Tibetan antique furniture. His *A Buyer's Guide to Chinese Furniture* is due out shortly.

He has been involved with the American Chamber of Commerce for a number of years and is currently chairman of AMCHAM China.

■ ■ ■

United Technologies Corporation has been in China a long time. Two of its founding companies, Otis Elevators and Carrier Air-Conditioning, established operations in Shanghai in the first decade of this century. After an absence that began with the change of government in 1949, a joint venture was established by Otis in Tianjin, near Beijing, on the Gulf of Bohai, in 1984. There followed, in the late 1980s and early 1990s, rapid investment by UTC's other divisions, including Carrier Air-Conditioning; Pratt & Whitney; Pratt & Whitney Canada; and UT Automotive, which makes automobile parts. During this period, UTC invested $300 million in 23 joint ventures and one wholly foreign-owned enterprise (or WFOE, colloquially known as a "wooffy").

"To begin to understand how to operate in China," says Dr. Latham, "it helps to understand the differences between Chinese society and its people and the society and people you know back home. There is a Chinese way of looking at things and a Chinese way of doing things. However, this does not mean that the way you do business in China has to be entirely different from elsewhere. Every country is different, yet there are similarities. Unfortunately, too few executives who come to China have worked in many countries. They fail to realize that there are bureaucracies everywhere, that there are pollution and traffic jams, that the political and economic issues are remarkably the same, that there are trade barriers and complex social issues. So one has to understand where China is the same and where it differs and what impact these differences have, if any, on how one does business."

Having spent most of his career working with Chinese, Dr. Latham is well placed to identify the key differences from Western society and how they are relevant to the business environment. He points to four differences in support of his thesis that you must think from a Chinese perspective.

"First, there is the question of relationships. *Guanxi* (or relationships) is one of the first words a person learns when he or she comes to China. Anyone who has been around will tell you that networking and building relationships are important everywhere in the world. But newcomers here think that they have stumbled across something so entirely unique that only the Chinese are concerned with it. What is different about China is the intensity of preoccupation with relationship building, which goes on the whole time; it is an almost consuming aspect of Chinese life. Foreign managers fail to realize how pervasive it is, and that at every meeting, social or business, the Chinese participants are working on some aspect of the relationship.

"Another issue is the language, which is very different and can be difficult to learn. I don't want to overplay the importance of being able to speak and to read Chinese, although clearly it can be a useful tool. I recall a debate years ago at college between two professors, one of whom understood the Chinese language very well, while the other had no foreign language skills. They were walking through a bookstore when one commented to the other, 'Look, to prove my point, there's *The Dream of the Red Chamber* in English. So why do I have to get a Ph.D. in the Chinese language just to read it? It's there.' His Chinese-speaking colleague replied, 'That's true, but the English version of *The Dream of the Red Chamber* includes only about 40 percent of the novel.' It's the same with language in a factory. You can get by using English, but you may be missing 60 percent of what's going on. And that can't help but have an impact on productivity and the bottom line.

"The Chinese language is quite unlike European languages. There are no cognates—words of common origin, like *'porte'* in French, 'portal' in English. There are no common or similarly written words between Chinese and, say, English or German. I had a case in one joint venture where the financial and operating reports sent in English to the foreign manager showed different numbers than the Chinese-language reports issued to the Chinese manager. The foreign manager couldn't read the headings and the columns, so the Chinese partner had a better understanding of what was going on in the factory than the foreign factory manager."

Dr. Latham highlights a third important difference, namely the absence of intermediary organizations in Chinese society. Unlike in Western countries, there are no business or social organizations such as Masonic lodges and Rotary Clubs. Alumni associations and cultural groups are only just beginning to be established. Because of this, there are no intervening institutions between the state and the individual, who has only his or her workplace to turn to for support. Traditionally, the work unit has provided everything, and the Chinese have come to expect paternalistic treatment from their factory in terms of housing, medical care, schooling, even arranged marriages; this is what is known as the "iron rice bowl."

Dr. Latham continues, "In a Chinese entity, the manager will take time to visit people who are in the hospital. He will visit older employees who have retired. There's a very personal touch to it. And we, the foreigners, are by and large unable to do that. So employees continue to turn to the Chinese manager for many things because they receive that emotional comfort. I'm not saying that foreign-invested enterprises have to go completely Chinese in this respect. But we need to understand what the social dynamics are in the minds of Chinese employees. And we cannot easily change the expectations of the employees about their relationships with their Chinese managers."

The expectation that the Chinese partner in a Sino-foreign joint venture will take care of employees accounts partly for the great importance given to the issue of "control" in joint-venture discussions. Dr. Latham points out that the key concerns of the foreigner relate to control of the technology, the quality of the product, and the financial information. The Chinese, on the other hand, want to control the workforce, in keeping with the traditional manner in which organizations in the PRC are controlled. Often fearing that the foreign partner will seek to cut a large workforce, the Chinese managers don't want to abrogate their responsibility. In return for this control, the Chinese partner provides care for the employees.

Every senior executive charged with the task of building a business in China is acutely aware of the importance of training. In highlighting a fourth difference, Dr. Latham puts a new spin on the subject. "A Chinese who had worked abroad once pointed out to me that Western society is a digital society, whereas Chinese society is an analog society. To give you an example: When a Westerner walks into a room, he begins unconsciously to check what the wallpaper is like, to look at the cornice, the woodwork, the way the windows are constructed, the character of furnishings. He takes in every little detail as he builds a picture of what the room is like. When a Chinese walks into a room, if it looks the way a room should look, he's content. It's a room, period.

"There is a similar phenomenon in Chinese art. By and large, when a human being is depicted in a Chinese landscape painting, the form isn't rendered in excruciating detail, as you often find in traditional Western painting. The Chinese will look at it and say, 'Ah, that's a mountain, that's a forest, and there's a human being.' Mood and analogy are more important than details.

"This difference has unusual consequences when it comes to technology. We can bring into a joint venture factory a technology model of how to produce something. Our Chinese partners will try to copy the model exactly. But the result will be an analogous copy, because they will look at it with eyes that are accustomed to seeing analogies. They will miss the detail and not understand why things are done in a certain way. To look at the issue conversely, a Westerner introduced to chopsticks for the first time typically doesn't know how to grasp and smoothly manipulate them, without training. To come back to the point: The way we train in China is important, because the implicit logic, often culturally based, isn't always apparent and understood. We go back to basics and question our own assumptions about what is self-evident. And we keep training and retraining."

These were new insights into some of the differences between Chinese and Western society and the impact of those differences on doing business in China. But I wanted to take the debate on to the next stage. "What, in your view," I asked Dr. Latham, "are the key success factors?"

"Three come to mind right away," he responded. "First, successfully integrating Chinese culture and Western technology is key. It has been said that 'the message is the medium.' In our joint ventures, where we have taken the message and wrapped it in Chinese paper, we have succeeded very well in changing ideas and work habits.

"For example, the Chinese like to see messages, usually two lines of characters, on a wall. Large posters are a tradition, sometimes related to auspicious dates or anniversaries. In a number of our factories, the managers have taken key company messages, arranged for someone with a fine hand to put them into couplets and write them out, and then hung them on the wall. The result has been significant. By delivering messages in this way, the interface between management and the workforce has been much smoother.

"Take another example. At Carrier we wanted to introduce quality control measures. Management got the workers involved in statistical processes, and over the course of four or five years, very substantial improvements in worker productivity were achieved, but not by working longer hours; in fact, we had less overtime. Productivity kept increasing in multiples, not just small percentages, to the point that a year or so ago, workers and technicians from those factories were sent to our other factories in Asia to teach productivity improvement. One of the keys to this achievement was extensive involvement of the trade union. We made it clear to union leaders why we were doing each thing. Once they understood the positive impact on employees, we found that instead of resisting change they helped to ensure that the walls came tumbling down. Employees saw that they were going to be clear beneficiaries of the process changes. In the end, the quality of living of employees improved; the quality of the product improved; and productivity went up without having to increase the size of the workforce. We were able to achieve all this at Carrier because we had some managers who were bicultural and bilingual. They communicated well, not just linguistically, but by really understanding how the Chinese think about these subjects."

Dr. Latham provides another example to make his point. "The Chinese are very eager to get the latest technology in the world. But there is a typical misperception on their part that technology is value-free. They don't appreciate that technology has an impact on society, culture, and ways of working. Sometimes values that are, in fact, part and parcel of a technology are considered to be foreign. As a result, the Chinese may tend to reject it. So we have to work hard. We have to help our employees distinguish between foreign practices and values, and those values that stem inherently from the technology."

A second key success factor suggested by Dr. Latham can be summarized under the maxim, "Do your homework and ask the right questions." As chairman of AMCHAM China, he meets a large number of foreign executives. "When I listen to managers from all sorts of companies, I'm often surprised by how nebulous their goals and objectives are before they come to China. They form partnerships and then can't figure out why they did it. Probably, the truth of the matter is they didn't give much thought to it in the beginning. They didn't do their homework. You know, it's amazing that many times companies don't know what questions to ask. The Chinese will answer precisely the questions they are asked. But they usually won't volunteer answers to fill in the gaps, and they won't think about the questions the foreigner didn't ask. They take the view that the foreigner must know what he is doing."

This issue of companies' not undertaking comprehensive due diligence before committing to a relationship and to expenditure in China is a significant factor in the failure of many international corporations in China. The country is more complicated than others. It is not one market, but many. About 40 percent of Sino-foreign joint ventures are loss-making, and after a while international companies try to buy out Chinese partners with whom they cannot easily get along.

Dr. Latham's third key success factor is *localization*. The topic is a priority for foreign corporations. As he remarks, "It's the coin of the realm. It's on everyone's lips. If you talk about localization, it makes you politically correct. But when you get down to the real nuts and bolts, it is often honored in the breach. What drives localization, of course, is the cost of employing expatriates in China, and that's an important consideration. But you don't just want a lower-cost employee, you want a competent local employee. The Chinese are interested in localization for a reason of their own: career progress for Chinese employees. The priority is clear and shared, but the process does not lend itself to a rigid timetable.

"Another factor is the fierce desire on the part of the Chinese to be in control of their factories. On more than one occasion, I have offered the view that their ambitions are set too low; they should aspire to be regional or divisional presidents. Our businesses are led by nationals from all over the world, and we need to develop executives who can work across boundaries."

These three success factors apply, in Dr. Latham's view, to most businesses operating in China. There is a fourth success factor that he applies specifically to UTC's products, namely, the issue of maintaining quality. An area that merits special quality control procedures is the manufacture of Pratt & Whitney aircraft engine parts. They must meet FAA certification standards in an industry where there is no room for bogus or low-quality parts. In UTC's joint ventures in China, international quality controls must be applied. There is no alternative.

Dr. Latham's concern for both Carrier air conditioners and Otis elevators is with the quality of after-sales service and support. He points out, "When you're in an elevator and you see the name Otis on the panel, you have certain expectations about the performance of that elevator. What you will not find in the elevator is a sign saying that the elevator is maintained by the building owner or some other company in the elevator maintenance business. So if you have a bad ride, you blame Otis. As a result, Otis wants, as far as possible, to ensure that it is very strongly involved in after-sales service maintenance, so that the reputation of its product quality is maintained."

For years, China was regarded as a low-cost, low-quality environment, but that is changing—and UTC, among others, is helping to achieve that change. As Dr. Latham puts it, "If you have a properly run joint venture, you can manufacture parts in China just as well as you can in the United States, the UK, or France. The difference in the quality of the products is not that great in many cases. However, the path by which you get there exercises the mind. And to be successful in a Chinese factory, you have to acquire the skill of looking at production problems through Chinese eyes to discover how to make imported technologies and processes work."

United Technologies Corporation in China

UTC has global revenues of over US$25 billion, based on sales from the following operations: Pratt & Whitney and Sikorsky (aircraft engines); Hamilton Standard (environmental control systems for aircraft; space suits; and propellers); Otis Elevators and Carrier

Air-Conditioning; and UT Automotive (automobile parts), recently acquired by Lear. In 1999, Sundstrand will join the UTC family.

In China, UTC has 23 joint ventures and a wholly foreign-owned enterprise, Otis China Limited. Having invested over US$300 million, the corporation now manufactures and sells products in Beijing, Chengdu, Guangzhou, Jing de zheng, Shanghai, Tianjin, Xi'an, and Zhuzhou. Annual turnover amounts to approximately US$1 billion.

Index

About the Author

John Stuttard spent just over five years as Chairman and Chief Executive of the China business of Coopers & Lybrand and, since the global merger on 1 July 1998, of PricewaterhouseCoopers China.

After graduating in Economics from Cambridge University he taught English for a year with Voluntary Service Overseas in Borneo, where he also read the evening news on Radio Brunei and directed a production of Oscar Wilde's *The Importance of Being Earnest*. He then embarked on a career in accountancy, qualifying as a U.K.-chartered accountant in 1970, before becoming a partner in the London office of Coopers & Lybrand.

His career has been mostly spent assisting multinational corporations in achieving their cross-border ambitions. He has acted as reporting accountant to numerous stock exchange listings and has helped companies acquire and sell businesses in other countries. His longstanding interest in education and training resulted in his being appointed a director of the Cambridge University Appointments Board in the late 1970s. He also spent two years in the U.K. Cabinet Office Think Tank, advising the Government on the management and privatization of the U.K.'s nationalized industries. During the 1980s, he worked for many Scandinavian companies, and for his services to Finnish industry, in 1995 he was made a Knight First Class of the Order of the Lion of Finland.

Outside work, he is a keen collector of old cars that he rallies. A frequent entrant of the Monte Carlo Rallye de Voitures Anciennes, he has also been a Concours winner at Pebble Beach, California. In 1997 he drove his 1934 Rolls-Royce, painted pink as a result of sponsorship and coverage by the *Financial Times,* on the 10,000-mile journey from Peking to Paris. The Rolls-Royce Enthusiasts Club published his account of the successful adventure and he subsequently gave the twenty-first-anniversary lecture on this epic journey for the Sir Henry Royce Foundation.

Over the last five years, in China, he has built a business of professional accountants and advisers from 60 in 1994 to over 1,200, operating from Beijing, Shanghai, Guangzhou, Shenzhen, and Dalian. He has played a leading role helping to develop the CPA profession in China and has been honored by the Minister of Finance for his contribution to the training of accountants in the PRC.